Leading Successful PMOs

To my PMO compadres; Jan, Paul, Rob, Matthias, Kevin and Karl, it has been fun!

And to all those who contributed to this book through articles, comments, reviews and survey responses – a cast of thousands (well one thousand at least) – thank you! It is great to share the blame ...

Leading Successful PMOs

How to Build the Best Project Management Office for Your Business

PETER TAYLOR

Routledge
Taylor & Francis Group

LONDON AND NEW YORK

First published 2011 by Gower Publishing

Published 2016 by Routledge
2 Park Square, Milton Park, Abingdon, Oxon OX14 4RN
711 Third Avenue, New York, NY 10017, USA

Routledge is an imprint of the Taylor & Francis Group, an informa business

British Library Cataloguing in Publication Data
Taylor, Peter.
    Leading successful PMOs: how to build the best project
    management office for your business.
    1. Project management. 2. Project managers.
    I. Title
    658.4'04-dc22

Library of Congress Cataloging-in-Publication Data
Taylor, Peter.
    Leading successful PMOs : how to build the best project management
office for your business / Peter Taylor.
        p. cm.
    Includes bibliographical references and index.
    ISBN 978-1-4094-1837-5 (hardback : alk. paper) –
    ISBN 978-1-4094-1838-2 (ebook : alk. paper)
    1. Project management. 2. Leadership. I. Title.

    HD69.P75T3954 2011
    658.4'04–dc23

                                                              2011021028

ISBN 13: 978-1-4094-1837-5 (hbk)

Printed in the United Kingdom
by Henry Ling Limited

Contents

About the Author

Peter is a dynamic and commercially astute professional who has achieved notable success in Project Management.

His background is in project management across three major business areas over the last 26 years. He has worked with MRP/ERP systems with various software houses, within Business Intelligence (BI) with Cognos, and within product lifecycle management (PLM) with Siemens. He has spent the last seven years leading PMOs and developing project managers and is now focusing on project-based services development with Infor.

He is also an accomplished communicator and leader and is a professional speaker as well as the author of *The Lazy Project Manager*

(Infinite Ideas), *Leading Successful PMOs* (Gower) and *The Lazy Winner* (Infinite Ideas).

More information can be found at www.thelazyprojectmanager.com – and through his free podcasts on iTunes.

THE LAZY PROJECT MANAGER BOOK

The *Lazy Project Manager* illustrates how anyone can apply the simple techniques of lazy project management to their own activities in order to work more effectively and consequently improve work–life balance. This 'productive laziness' approach builds on the Pareto principle that states that for many phenomena, 80 per cent of consequences stem from 20 per cent of the causes. To put it simply, only 20 per cent of the things people do during their working days really matter.

Inside this book readers can discover:

- the intelligence of laziness – why smart, lazy people have the edge over others;

- why *The Jungle Book*'s 'Bare Necessities' should be the productive lazy theme tune;

- how to get the maximum output for a minimized input;

- quick tips to productive lazy heaven.

In addition, the author provides some interesting (and entertaining) things about eating dinosaurs, wearing ermine cloaks and how to spot a psychopathic woman at a funeral. The reader will find out why you should never go ballooning, how to deliver a good Oscar acceptance speech and why it is important for your team that you read the newspaper each morning.

And yes, you may also learn some, quick, simple but important things about project management.

ISBN: 978-1-9068-2113-5

WANT TO FIND OUT MORE?

If you would like to find out more about:

- Peter Taylor

- Project Management

- PMOs

- *The Lazy Project Manager*

- My Blogs

- My podcasts

Then just go to www.thelazyprojectmanager.com and www.thelazywinner.com for a whole lot more information, advice and generally pretty useful stuff.

Foreword

Chris Walters

Twenty years ago, when I first got my hands dirty in managing projects, the term 'PMO' didn't seem to exist. Attending a course on project management started to give me the tools to do the job I was entrusted with, and there was a very brief mention of a concept called 'project support', albeit brushed aside quickly as a luxury that real project managers (no doubt the 'eats girders for breakfast' type) could do without.

Coming back to the office, brimming with new concepts and strong resolve, I started to ask around for the infrastructure and templates that surely must have already been created. Some of that resolve turned to 'dissolve' as the stark realization hit home – if I wanted infrastructure, I (remember, still a novice project manager) would have to create them all myself. If only there was a PMO I could have gone to …

Fast forwarding to today then, the PMO is now a widely used acronym, and many companies doing more than a couple of projects have a PMO in place. PMOs are also widely understood, and indeed there is a framework (P3O) from the same stable as arguably the most widely used project management framework, PRINCE2.

Although the visible part of the PMO is often operational in nature, the real value of a PMO is when it becomes transformational. This is where leadership becomes much more important than management.

Peter's book breaks new ground in looking at the leadership of PMOs. True, there is a smattering of management topics too, to make sure that the day-to-day work of the PMO is neither neglected nor delivered inefficiently. But the thrust is about the right components of leadership required to not just change with the times, but to lead from the front and ensure that only the right projects are selected, they are delivered reliably and that the overall outcomes of the portfolio improve measurably over time.

The role of the PMO leader is one for a particular breed of individual. Be clear: this is a very senior position in any organization that takes project delivery seriously – the days of coordinating project administrators are over. PMO people are smart, articulate, expert, influential and business-focused these days, and they need a clear vision and strong leadership to thrive – the PMO leader has to provide this for them to be valuable. It's not enough to be inward-looking though, the PMO leader has to be an entrepreneur within their organization, selling PMO capability and delivering upon promises. It's all a finely-tuned balancing act – operation versus innovation, leading versus aligning and accelerating versus consolidating – and leading is all about making those choices.

This book reflects on PMO leadership topics based on Peter's extensive experience in inventing and reinventing PMO functions in fast moving organizations. If you need a PMO (which you do, if you deliver projects) and you really care about your business (which I also assume you do), then you need a strong PMO leader. Reading this book will give you a fantastic vision for the role and the person that would fill it.

Chris Walters is the Chairman of the PMOSIG (http://pmosig.co.uk/) – the UK's only specialist interest group for all PMO practitioners. Through regular conferences and online interaction, PMOSIG is a great starting place for anybody leading or working in a PMO to share ideas, network and become professionally engaged.

Foreword

David Ayling-Smith

In this book Peter has provided an easy-to-read summary of the characteristics of a good PMO, the steps to build it and the characteristic to lead one. This is a useful and timely synopsis, as I suspect many organizations would benefit from a PMO but don't realize it yet or don't know how to start.

I have worked with Peter building two differently focused PMOs in the last ten years, and I am currently working with a third. Although the ambitions of each have not been the same, they all share similar positive characteristics which, from an executive sponsorship perspective, make them indispensible in my opinion.

Whichever sort of PMO you have, I believe that PMOs provide a vital role in driving alignment within an organization which accelerates organization improvement and change, often consolidating similarly focused activities that were previously competing for resources. It allows for simplification of process and better understanding of priorities. All this allows for a more engaged executive-supporting role that can accelerate decision making.

The supportive nature of the PMO should not be underestimated. There is the battle (and it is a battle) to make sense of a problem project and the nagging concern that there might be other similarly afflicted projects out there that you don't yet know about . Also the realization that you need to learn from your mistakes so this type of problem doesn't happen again all fit squarely within the scope of your PMO.

At times of growth (or retrenchment) a correctly positioned PMO is a crusading banner under which projects are helped, improvements are delivered, strategy is made real and your people are developed in a way that aligns with corporate goals.

However, it is a journey, there is always something else to be done and understanding the level of maturity of your PMO is an important principle. The gradual evolution of the PMO towards a defined goal is a very positive phenomenon and you can celebrate small wins and continually communicate success to help adoption. In contrast, where the PMO does not have a clearly articulated objective, it is vulnerable to the Yellow Brick Road Syndrome – when you don't know where you are going all roads will tend to lead you there. Such a PMO becomes increasingly hard to direct and can be a divisive rather than harmonizing organization.

In the words (almost) of Reggie Perrin,[1] 'I wouldn't have got where I am today without a PMO.'

My experience of PMOs has been completely positive – helping unify strategic intentions with operational necessities – but it is a mission that requires a leadership rather than management approach. Because you are dealing with people and ideas and future states, it does not become real until someone says it is real and that person might just need to be you.

David Ayling-Smith has held executive-level positions in various software organizations. He has sponsored three PMOs across three industry leading companies over the last ten years.

---

1   Leonard Rossiter, who as the original Reginald Perrin, had the insufferable boss 'CJ', who started many lines with 'I didn't get where I am today...'

Acknowledgements

Many people contribute to a book like this so a big 'thank you' to all who put together a case study, who succumbed to my requests for interviews, who spent time completing the survey and who helped promote the survey itself, who joined in the various LinkedIn discussions and who just helped me on the journey. Your experience is way beyond my own and this book is all the better for your efforts.

Thanks also to my reviewers who took my rough draft to a level that was ready for the general publics' gaze. Without your efforts the public would have suffered so much more and so I am sure that they join me in thanking you.

Thank you also to my PMO team in Siemens PLM Software and to all of the project managers who work with my own and the other PMOs on those hundreds of customer projects – 'never letting our customers fail'.

Finally a big, big thank you to my family once more for allowing me the time to work on this project and neglect them.

Reviews for *Leading Successful PMOs*

For years there has been an inaccurate view that PMOs define and maintain project management standards. This view has led to untold PMO difficulties. The PMO in whatever shape or form is entirely about leadership and achievement. Kudos to Peter Taylor for spotlighting this and bringing us this practical reference.

Mark Price Perry, Founder, BOT International and author, *Business Driven PMO Setup* and *Business Driven PPM*

Finally a book for current and aspiring PMO leaders. While any practitioner worth his or her salt knows that the soft skills are what makes or breaks PMO leaders, too many organizations select their project leaders based on technical expertise. Whether you are charged with selecting the next PMO leader, aspiring to be one, or simply struggling to rise to the challenge of your leadership position Peter Taylor's insightful new work, Leading Successful PMOs, *will help set you on a focused path to leadership and success.*

J. LeRoy Ward, Executive Vice President, ESI International

Introduction

The PMO Acid Test

Call up your CEO and then count the number of seconds before he recognizes your name...

First in a series of quick checkpoints, or acid tests,[1] to see how successful the PMO you are leading is. If you are really connected to the business, at the right level and with the right profile, then your CEO will know you and your PMOs work.

INTRODUCTION

Leading Successful PMOs is a book to guide all would-be and current PMO (Project Management Office) leaders. As a PMO leader myself I know that this can be a really rewarding experience but it is not always easy to find the right balance between the needs of projects and business demands.

It is a book for all project-based organizations and for all project managers who contribute to and benefit from a PMO.

---

1 Acid test – a test used to determine whether a metal is real gold or not. Ever since, a generalized term for 'verified' or 'approved/tested'. In this case, a quick mental check on the state of your PMO.

It is a book about successfully leading a PMO (whatever you understand by those three letters) to deliver better projects, better business to all the customers of those projects and to best serve the contributing project managers professionally and personally.

It is not a book about *managing* PMOs but rather a book about *leading* PMOs; a complex challenge, especially in terms of reconciling the PMO activity with business strategy.

Leading Successful PMOs brings together the experience and views of PMO leaders from around the world; of project managers who work within PMOs, as well as those who are now seeking leaders for their PMOs.

I have tried to identify what it is that defines successful PMO leaders; what they do that allows them to be successful and how the rest of us can learn from their experiences. I have also tried to balance the value associated with the PMO value from the perspective of executives and the business as well as from that of PMO members, the project managers and supporting staff.

You can use the book as a health check against the PMO you are already leading or to assess your own contribution to the PMO; successful PMO leaders need a lot of support from their PMO teams so it is important that you understand what project managers are saying about PMOs.

Finally, I hope that *Leading Successful PMOs* will teach you how to lead the best, and most relevant, PMO for your business.

Leadership and learning are indispensable to each other.

John F. Kennedy

The PMO Acid Test

When was the last time that a project manager contacted your PMO asking for some form of help?

If this has not happened in some time then perhaps your PMO is not as accessible and open as you may wish it to be?

1 The Meaning and Purpose of a PMO

In this chapter we:

- explore the various definitions of PMOs;

- ensure that we all have a common understanding of what a PMO can (and can't) be; and

- appreciate who the stakeholders are likely to be; who it is who is most interested in your PMO being a success.

PMO 'JEOPARDY'?

Let me start in the spirit of that classic US game show 'Jeopardy!'[1] ...

Answer: 'A PMO.'

Question: (and therefore actually the correct answer; that is just the way it works on the game show, trust me – or look it up) 'What is the department or group that defines and maintains the standards of process, generally related to project management, within an organization?'

Applause from the audience and smiles all round.

---

1 'Jeopardy!' is an American quiz show featuring trivia in history, literature, the arts, pop culture, science, sports, geography, wordplay, and more. The show has a unique answer-and-question format in which contestants are presented with clues in the form of answers, and must phrase their responses in question form.

Yes, the Project Management Office (PMO) in a business or professional enterprise is typically the department or group that defines and maintains the standards of process, that are generally related to project management, within the organization.

But I am afraid it is not that simple.

The abbreviation, PMO, can stand for Programme Management Office (confusingly also a PMO) or Portfolio Management Office (increasingly confusingly also a PMO). There is even talk of a Project Office (PO), a Project Control Office (PCO), a Central Project Office (CPO), and a Project Support Office (PSO). Up to you to choose – what do you have in your company? What are you leading? What are you part of? What is it that you are currently planning?

You may well have a completely different flavour of PMO from the above.

The PMO strives to standardize and introduce economies of repetition in the execution of projects and is the source of documentation, guidance and metrics on the practice of project management and project execution.

It is also the body that links business strategy to the projects that such strategies require.

Organizations around the globe are defining, borrowing and collecting best practices in process and project management and are increasingly assigning the PMO to exert overall influence and evolution of thought to continual organizational improvement.

Many PMOs will base project management principles on accepted industry standard methodologies such as the PMBOK[2] or PRINCE2.[3]

There are as many variances in the structure, format and focus of PMOs as there are definitions of the term.

PMO Types

Typically there are five basic types of PMO:

1. a Departmental PMO

2. a Special-purpose PMO

3. an Outreaching PMO

4. an External PMO

5. an Enterprise PMO

It should also be noted: the 'enterprise' structure can apply in more than one of the first four categories.

Type definition aside, a PMO is a group or department within a business, agency or enterprise that 'owns' the kind of project-based activity that cuts across the operational activity. The primary goal of a PMO is to achieve benefits from standardizing and following project management policies, processes and methods. Over time, a PMO will become the source for guidance, documentation

---

2   The Project Management Body of Knowledge (PMBOK Guide) is a project management guide, and an internationally recognized standard that provides the fundamentals of project management as they apply to a wide range of projects, including construction, software, engineering, automotive, and so on. The purpose of the PMBOK is to provide and promote a common vocabulary within the project management profession for discussing, writing, and applying project management concepts. The PMBOK is developed by The Project Management Institute (PMI®) – a non-profit professional organization for the project management profession with the purpose of advancing project management

3   'PRojects IN Controlled Environments' (PRINCE) is a project management method. It covers the management, control and organisation of a project. PRINCE2 refers to the second major version of this method and is a registered trademark of the Office of Government Commerce (OGC), an independent office of HM Treasury of the United Kingdom.

and metrics related to the practices involved in managing and implementing projects within that organization.

WHY INVEST?

Why do businesses invest in a PMO?

On the one hand, companies of all kinds face the continued fallout from the most recent global recession which has placed an added burden on projects and project managers delivering expected benefits.

On the other, we are part of a dynamic, resourceful and ever-evolving commercial world that demands change as part of its survival; change demands projects, and projects demand project managers.

History is littered with significant project failures (witness some of the statistics of the CHAOS[4] report analysis of IT project success, and more often failure[5]), yet there are also spectacular project success stories linked to the maturing practice of project management.

Those projects that will be commissioned in the future, as well as the ones that are allowed to continue in the current challenging climate, will be expected to deliver greater business benefits, endure closer scrutiny from senior management and are likely to face far more pressures to deliver. There is no longer any room for project failure; projects that are approved need to succeed.

---

4   The Standish Group regularly produces the CHAOS reports which research the reasons for IT project failure in the United States, the last report showed that software projects now have a 32 per cent success rate, or put it another way, a 68 per cent chance of 'failure'. As an example of 'failure' the Standish Group found that the average cost overrun was 43 per cent; 71 per cent of projects were over budget, exceeded time estimates, and had estimated too narrow a scope; and total waste was estimated at $55 billion per year in the US alone.

5   The Standish Group report has been challenged in the past. With the problem being that it measures success by only looking at whether the projects were completed on time, on budget and with the required features and functions. It does not address such other measures of the quality, the risk, and customer satisfaction. Nevertheless we can all speak to a project success score of less than 100 per cent.

And who will be under the most pressure? You guessed it, the managers responsible for those projects.

Right now our projects, and our project managers, need the help, support and guidance of a good PMO and a 'good' PMO has to be led by a 'good' PMO leader.

The good news is that PMOs are in demand.

In their 'The State of the PMO 2010'[6] report, PM Solutions stated that: 'The upward trend is unmistakable, both in sheer numbers of PMOs and in the rising organizational clout. In our 2000 research on "The Value of Project Management", only 47 per cent of companies had a project office. In 2006, our research on "Project Management: The State of the Industry" showed that 77 per cent of companies had PMOs; "The State of the PMO 2010" research shows that 84 per cent of companies have PMOs.'

9

This is excellent news; it suggests the battle to establish the value of the PMO has, for the most part, been won.

This book is therefore less about the business justification of a PMO and more about being the very best that you can be as a leader and a contributor to a successful PMO; making your PMO the one that really delivers.

PROGRAMS, PROGRAMMES AND PMOS

To avoid confusion, it is important that we all have a common understanding of project and PMO terminology.

To that end we should all align our language when it comes to Projects and Programmes,[7] Portfolios and PMOs.

---

6   PM Solutions Research (2010). 'The State of the PMO 2010'. Research report. Glen Mills, PA: PM Solutions: www.pmsolutions.com.

7   The basic difference is between different languages: American English always uses program – British English uses programme unless referring to computers. Australian English recommends program for official usage, but programme is still in common use. The word 'program' was predominant in the UK until the nineteenth

It can be a very confusing world when we talk of projects and programmes and portfolios and PMOs so I am going to open with the simplest of explanations which I am hoping you will accept for the purposes of this book.

Portfolio
• Doing the right things

Project
• Doing it the right way

Programme
• Doing it in the right order

PMO
• Doing it all with right team

Project Management is all about doing something (a project) in the right way and the 'right way' is all about method and discipline and quality and control.

Programme Management is all about doing those things (the projects) in the right sequence or order.

Portfolio Management is about doing the right things.

Which leaves the PMO; and which I think of as doing all the above but with the right team (the right things, in the right way, in the right order).

Hopefully that helps.

---

century, when the spelling 'programme' became more common – largely as a result of influence from French, which has the same word 'programme'.

If you prefer a more detailed explanation:

Project management

Project management is the discipline of planning, organizing, securing and managing resources to bring about the successful completion of specific project goals and objectives. It is sometimes confused with programme management, however technically that is actually a higher-level construction: a group of related and interdependent projects.

A project is a temporary endeavour, having a defined beginning and end (usually constrained by date, but can be by funding or deliverables), undertaken to meet unique goals and objectives, usually to bring about beneficial change or added value. The temporary nature of projects stands in contrast to business as usual (or operations), which are repetitive, permanent or semi-permanent functional work to produce products or services. In practice, the management of these two systems is often found to be quite different, and as such requires the development of distinct technical skills and the adoption of separate management.

The primary challenge of project management is to achieve all of the project goals and objectives while honouring the preconceived project constraints, or at least in managing the adjustments of these constraints through a disciplined process. Typical constraints are scope, time and budget together with an over-arching consideration of quality.

Programme management

Programme management is the process of managing several related projects, often with the intention of improving an organization's performance. A programme of projects can help a company achieve one or more of its strategies. The individual projects within it have varying end dates but the programme ends when the strategy has been reached.

There are two different views of how programmes differ from projects.

In one view, projects deliver outputs, discrete parcels or 'chunks' of change; programmes create outcomes. Thus, a project might deliver a new factory, hospital or IT system. By combining these projects with other deliverables and changes, the associated programme might deliver increased income from a new product, shorter waiting lists at the hospital or reduced operating costs due to improved technology.

The alternative view is that a programme is nothing more than either a large project or a set of projects. In this second view, the point of a programme is to exploit economies of scale and to reduce coordination costs and risks. The project manager's job is to ensure that their project succeeds. The programme manager, on the other hand, may not care about individual projects, but is concerned with the aggregate result or end-state. For example, in a financial institution a programme may include one project that is designed to take advantage of a rising market, and another to protect against the downside of a falling market. These apparently opposing projects fit together in the same programme.

Portfolio management

Project portfolio management (sometimes referred to as PPM) is a management process designed to help an organization to register and view information about all of its projects. Once it has the visibility (you can't manage what you don't measure) then this allows such organizations to sort and prioritize each project according to certain criteria, such as:

- strategic value

- cost

- impact on resources

- tactical need

A PPM-driven organization will have, typically, a portfolio/project dashboard representing the overall health and status of each project.

It should be noted that the projects and/or programmes within a given portfolio may not necessarily be interdependent or directly related to each other. For example, in a services-supplying company the portfolio will mainly record customer project activity with little relationship between the individual projects.

PMOs

The PMO in a business or professional enterprise is the department or group that defines and maintains the standards of the business processes, generally related to project management. The PMO strives to standardize and introduce economies of repetition in the execution of projects. The PMO is the source of documentation, guidance and metrics on the practice of project management and execution.

A good PMO will base project management principles on accepted, industry standard methodologies, as well as government regulatory requirements as applicable. Organizations around the globe are defining, borrowing and collecting best practices in process and project management and are increasingly assigning the PMO to exert overall influence and evolution of thought to continual organizational improvement.

Establishing a PMO group is not a short-term strategy to lower costs. Recent surveys indicate that the longer organizations have an operating PMO group the better the results achieved to accomplish project goals (which might lead to eventually lowering costs).

PMOs may take other functions beyond standards and methodology, and participate in strategic project management either as facilitator or actively as owner of the portfolio management process. Tasks may include monitoring and reporting on active projects (following up project until completion), and reporting progress to top management for strategic decisions on what projects to continue or cancel.

So there you have it – personally I like my simple model better so let's stick to that shall we?

A simple guide

Copy the PMO declaration and put it up on your office wall – it will help.

The PMO is all about doing it all but with the right team, but as there is no one model for a PMO you'll not be surprised that there is no one 'right' team to make up the PMO.

Being a successful PMO leader is all about delivering the 'right stuff'[8] and putting together the right team to do this. There is a lot more to this as just having the 'right team' doing 'the right job' is no guarantee of success. But we will explore this idea a lot more later on in the book. Being part of a PMO team is all about supporting the 'right stuff' delivery by best practice and professionalism. By being a leader of a successful PMO.

The PMO Leader = The Right Stuff

Your PMO; doing the right things, in the right way, in the right order, with the right team

---

---

8   *The Right Stuff* is a 1979 book by Tom Wolfe about the pilots engaged in US postwar experiments with experimental rocket-powered, high-speed aircraft as well as documenting the stories of the first Project Mercury astronauts selected for the NASA space programme. The story contrasts the 'Mercury Seven' and their families with test pilots such as Chuck Yeager, who was considered by many contemporaries as the best of them all, but who was never selected as an astronaut. Wolfe wrote that the book was inspired by the desire to find out why the astronauts accepted the danger of space flight. He recounts the enormous risks that test pilots were already taking, and the mental and physical characteristics—the titular 'right stuff'—required for and reinforced by their jobs. Wolfe likens the astronauts to 'single combat warriors' from an earlier era who received the honour and adoration of their people before going forth to fight on their behalf. There was also a film in 1982 based on the book.

YOUR VERY OWN DING IN THE UNIVERSE[9]

There are many dimensions to the PMO; different types of PMOs; PMO styles of behaviour, and there are permanent PMOs and temporary PMOs. There are PMOs that direct project managers and there are PMOs which only influence project managers.

Consider this the universe of the PMO, or at least the potential universe. Clearly in each of your organizations you will only have elements of the full PMO universe – this will be your own PMO world, your own 'ding'.

It is important to understand the potential range of PMO activity as is it may influence your project strategy and open your eyes to what more your own PMO might support.

Let's begin with what a PMO can be.

What can a PMO be?

A PMO can typically be one of five types from an organizational perspective:

1. a departmental PMO

2. a special-purpose PMO

3. an outreaching (supplier) PMO

4. an external (customer) PMO

5. and there is the model of an enterprise PMO.

There is one view that there are only three PMO types: enterprise, departmental and special-purpose. However, it is easy to overlook those organizations that run PMOs to support project managers working alongside and managing customer-led projects for external clients.

---

9   When he was a young man and Apple was still just finding its feet, Steve Jobs told a TV reporter: 'I want to make a ding in the universe.' And you know what? He has.

If you are a service-based company you will certainly recognize this flavour of the PMO. These externally-focused PMOs may be involved in advising and supporting customer-centred PMOs – offering governance, guidance and resources.

So I believe that there are in fact six types of PMO.

A way of looking at this is to consider 'internal' PMOs – those PMOs that oversee projects that are sanctioned within an organization for self-improvement or compliance reasons – as one category.

'External' PMOs – those PMOs that exist to ensure that an organizations' customer projects deliver the return on investment expected – are a second category.

A third category can be the 'special-purpose' PMOs created for specific situations or needs. For example, a PMO might be created to assist in an acquisition process to contribute to the due diligence process and to aid the integration post-acquistion.

A further dimension is the scale of the PMO; from departmental or business unit level through to enterprise level.

Internal PMOs

Let's begin with perhaps the most common type of PMO; the internal PMO that is focused on projects primarily within its own parent organization, for self-improvement or compliance purposes.

The most common variety of these will be the departmental PMO.

Department-based PMOs may simply be a small group that manages very specific projects within their own landscape and with their own resources. The limitations of such a PMO are that any projects that require resources outside the department may have difficulties securing and maintaining such resources due to pressures from their own department's priorities.

External PMOs

Now let's consider those PMOs that are not internal to an organization but that focus on the outside customers of many service companies, for example, or support other parts of a group operation.

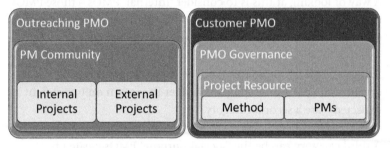

The Outreaching (Supplier) PMO can offer the Customer PMO guidance in PMO set up and PMO Governance as well as resources from the (Supplier) PM Community

Outreaching (supplier) PMO

In this situation, the PMO's role is to oversee project methodology and practice and standards for a community of project managers dealing with projects outside of their own organization. Typically these projects take place at external organizations or other parts of a group of companies. The outreaching PMO has a set of skills that they can offer (sell) to the deploying company to aid them in their project work.

Beyond just offering project managers to these external companies, the PMO can also offer other services such as:

- governance consultancy;

- PMO initiation and evolvement;

- development of the customer's project managers and project teams in project skills and methodology;

- quality assurance activities to aid de-risking of project work;

- lessons learned process; and

- audits and health checks.

This is a common role when deploying solutions developed by their own company as a supplier to these external customers.

External (customer) PMO

In this situation the outreaching PMO will ideally interconnect with the external, or customer's own, PMO to provide a seamless and simple means of communication that will allow for the optimum:

- allocation of resources;

- best practice adoption;

- project tracking;

- escalation;

- cost management; and

- commercial relationship.

For large and multi-country/multi-division/global organizations working together on project-based work, a 'PMO to PMO' engagement model will offer the most effective operational structure.

Enterprise PMOs

For both the internal and the external PMOs there can be large benefits in scaling up to an enterprise level.

- Enterprise internal PMO: Operating at a corporate level allows the PMO to gain a strategic position within the organization and to ensure that projects proceed based on their strategic alignment to the key business objectives of that organization. Such an enterprise PMO is far more likely to gain executive support due its perceived (and actual) role in delivering strategy than a departmental one which does not connect with the executive in any direct way.

- Enterprise external PMO: Equally an 'outreaching' PMO may move up to the corporate level. This allows the 'outreaching' PMO to gain a strategic position within its own organization and offers external customers a consistent project delivery and service model wherever they are across the world.

Special-purpose PMOs

In some cases there may be a need for special PMOs created for a specific and discrete purpose.

- Special-purpose PMO: In this instance, the PMO may be departmental or enterprise focused and may be IT and/ or business focused. It will, however, be created only for a special purpose and will, most likely, cease to exist once that purpose has been completed.

Operational mode

So far we have explored one dimension of the PMO; the internal or external focus of its work. Now let's explore the second dimension – that of operating method or approach.

A PMO can operate in a number of ways:

- supportive

- controlling

- directive

Supportive

The supportive PMO aims to help out project managers by providing a level of support in the form of templates, guidelines, best practices, knowledge and project expertise; typically based on personal experience and often involving a network of experienced people throughout the organization.

Creating a supportive PMO involves bringing together a project community, where previously there may only have been silos of project-based activity and little knowledge sharing.

Why use a supporting model?

- simply to aid the existing project activity in order to raise the levels of project success;

- to share project management information across a wider group of project managers; and

- to empower project managers and project teams to solve common problems and become more successful.

Controlling

The controlling PMO is appropriate where there is a desire to have a stronger discipline across all project activities, methods, procedures and documentation.

Why use a controlling model?

- to ensure that a standard and consistent methodology is used;

- to ensure regulatory compliance;

- in cases where there are regular reviews that need to be passed;

- for a project or projects that are higher risk or higher profile; or

- for a new business endeavour.

Directive

The directive PMO governs the project or projects by providing the requisite project management experience and resources.

Project managers are assigned to each new project from the PMO itself and progress reporting is directed to the PMO.

Why use a directive model?

- to guarantee the highest level of consistency of project management practice across all projects;

- to reduce costs by centralizing project services; and

- to de-risk project delivery.

Each of the three models can be effective in different situations, depending upon what is required by the project landscape and the management. A supportive model does not allow for any direct ownership to take place, and a directive model requires ownership of the project management resources.

It is also very possible that, over time and as the project activity matures, an organization will move through the various models.

Because of this the most common model seen is actually a blended variant of all three models.

Blended

There is another way that PMOs can operate and that is a combination; a mixture of directive, supporting and controlling, better described as a 'blended' approach. The blend may involve any two modes or a combination of all three.

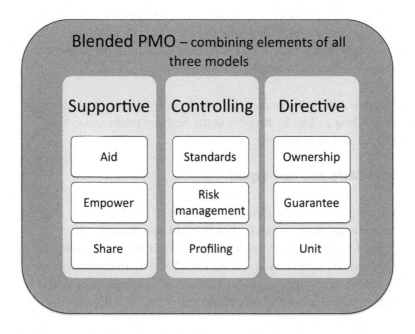

As you will see later on from my own survey of project managers and PMO leaders (page 74), 26 per cent of the PMOs I interviewed operate in a blended manner, so this is a relatively common PMO mechanism – offering flexibility according to the actual and individual need.

My own PMO is an example of this. Our default stance is to provide support to project managers and project communities as and when they need it. In order to do this we are responsible for the methodology, training and standards for project management and offer all of these as a framework for project managers. So we are a supportive PMO.

However, for some projects, for example if we are under the constraints of a fixed price contract or the project is of a particularly high risk category, then the PMO will be more controlling. This implies requiring adherence to more of our methodology, higher-quality management levels and the use of more detailed reporting of the project status through the PMO.

Finally, if there is a belief that a project is running out of control, the PMO may well sensibly step in and take a more direct role.

Perhaps with an initial action of the PMO leading a review or health check and, potentially, then taking management of the project in order to lead a successful recovery plan.

In this way we operate a model that flexes from supportive through controlling and on to directive as the business needs and as the individual projects require.

All PMOs are not equal

We have discussed the dimension of 'type of PMO' and of 'operational mode of PMO', now let's add the dimension of 'maturity of PMO' in to our increasingly complex PMO model. All PMO leaders should try and move their PMO up the maturity scale to a level that is appropriate and relevant to the organization that is funding and sponsoring that PMO:

> Level 1: Ad hoc – Where the project discipline has few, if any, formal definitions and is performed on an ad hoc basis. The PMO will typically get involved as trouble shooters and recovery agents.

> Level 2: Defined – Where the project discipline is defined, executed and repeatable. Here the PMO will have set in place standards and methods and will measure adoption and compliance accordingly.

> Level 3: Controlled – Where the project discipline targets are aligned with business goals and defined with greater detail. Results are qualitatively predictable and the PMO will operate a governance model involving reporting and deviation correction.

> Level 4: Measured – Quantitative[10] goals are clearly set and measured. The PMO will lead the measurement of project

---

10 The term quantitative refers to a type of information based in quantities or else quantifiable data (objective properties) – as opposed to qualitative information which deals with apparent qualities (subjective properties).

behaviour through KPIs[11] and metrics requiring intervention by exception.

Level 5: Optimized – There is a focus on continually improving the discipline performance. The PMO moves beyond the individual project focus and looks more towards incremental and innovative changes/improvements. To this end the PMO may well initiate projects for self-improvement.

The organization at Level 1 is, I suggest, not really a PMO but rather some form of SWAT[12] team; a specialist group of senior, and therefore 'seen it and done it and lived to tell the tale' project managers who are available to troubleshoot projects.

The true PMO appears at maturity Level 2: Defined.

So what's the best solution?

Of course, there is no one correct solution. You choice of PMO should depend on your organization's needs and expectations, willingness to invest, structure, project culture and challenges.

There are some common themes, whatever model, type and maturity level you start with and eventually aim for. To go back to the metaphor, you need to create your own PMO ding in your own project universe.

---

11 A Performance Indicator or Key Performance Indicator (KPI) is an industry jargon term for a type of Measure of Performance. KPIs are commonly used by an organization to evaluate its success or the success of a particular activity in which it is engaged. Sometimes success is defined in terms of making progress toward strategic goals but often, success is simply the repeated achievement of some level of operational goal (zero defects, ten out of ten customer satisfaction, project delivery to time, to cost, to quality and so on). These assessments often lead to the identification of potential improvements; and as a consequence, performance indicators are routinely associated with 'performance improvement' initiatives. A very common method for choosing KPIs is to apply a management framework such as the Balanced Scorecard.

12 A SWAT (Special Weapons And Tactics) team is an elite paramilitary tactical unit in American law enforcement departments. They are trained to perform high-risk operations that fall outside of the abilities of regular officers. The first SWAT team was established in the Los Angeles Police Department in 1968. Here SWAT is used to describe a specialist team of experts used in special circumstances.

Any PMO will:

- implement some form of common project methodology, whether internally developed or externally acquired;

- standardize project terminology through such a methodology and project initiation;

- introduce effective and repeatable project management processes;

- develop, train and, perhaps, certify their project managers to a common standard – again whether internally developed or externally subscribed to; and

- provide common supporting tools.

And is it real?

Just when you thought that it couldn't get any more complicated I am afraid to say that it definitely can. For example, you might also wish to consider the concept of a 'virtual PMO'.

It may be that an organization feels that it does not have the experience or resources to run a successful PMO, or requires that its own dedicated staff have other priorities, or it actually wants to benefit from the value of a PMO but in a very short time span that doesn't fit in with developing and building one internally.

The virtual PMO could be the answer to this problem.

In the case of a virtual PMO, a third party supplies the requisite management, resources, skills and knowledge. The choice is then whether this the ongoing model for the PMO or whether this is an initial model, for the purpose of expediency and as part of the PMO's remit there is an objective to manage the transition of all PMO activity (and therefore skills and knowledge) inside the company at some point in the future.

WHAT DOES A PMO DO?

Finally, and just for completeness sake, let's take a very quick look at what a PMO does (or could do).

The short answer is 'anything that the business wants it to do' – especially if that PMO is trying to establish its role, credibility and value within the organization.

The longer answer could include:

- project management community or practice ownership or lead;

- methodology;

- training and certification;

- resource management;

- project (programme-portfolio) reporting;

- coaching, mentoring, support;

- business alignment;

- quality control;

- financial follow up and support; and

- project selection and/or decision making.

And much more besides. The PMO's range of responsibilities can be simple or complex.

Add to that the many forms of PMOs that can exist and it could be said that there is no single answer or solution to project and business challenges for which the PMO could be the answer.

AND THE QUESTION IS...

If you go back to our question and answer session in the style of 'Jeopardy!' from earlier in this chapter:

Answer: 'A PMO.'

Question: 'What is the department or group that defines and maintains the standards of process, generally related to project management, within the organization and that links business strategy to the projects that such strategies require?'

There does need to be a second question and answer:

Answer: 'Your specific PMO.'

Question: 'What is the department or group that defines and maintains the standards of process, generally related to project management, and is customized to the current and planned requirements of that organization to deliver immediate business benefits and aid project success?'

And that leads to a third question and answer (naturally):

Answer: 'Anything that you would like it to do.'

Question: 'What will this PMO do?'

Congratulations – you are a winner!

ME, ME AND NOT FORGETTING ME

Let's take a moment to explore who the likely PMO Stakeholders are. Who is it that is most interested in and who benefits from a PMO? Equally, who might be threatened by the creation of a PMO?

There can be many and varied stakeholders; but here are a few to think about:

- Board members;

- executive team;

- business unit leaders/operational managers;

- project sponsors;

- programme managers/project managers/project administrators;

- programme/project team members;

- customers;

- partners; and

- don't forget yourself as the PMO leader.

A stakeholder is a person, group, organization or system who affects or can be affected by an action, and in this case that action is your leadership of a PMO.

The aim of stakeholder management is to gain influential support towards achieving your personal and/or business objectives. You do this by creating positive relationships with stakeholders through the appropriate management of their expectations and (agreed) objectives.

It's worth taking a moment just to reiterate the basic management process:

- Stakeholder identification:

  - start by mapping out your stakeholders – don't limit your thinking, anyone and everyone who uses, needs or is affected by the PMO is a stakeholder.

- Stakeholder analysis:

    - next you need to recognize and acknowledge your stakeholder's needs, concerns, wants, authority, relationships and interfaces.

- Stakeholder matrix or power/influence map:

    - now you need to consider each stakeholders combined power and influence so that you can plan your management approach.

- Stakeholder engagement:

    - here is the opportunity to discuss and agree expectations of communication and responsibility.

- Communication:

    - always maintain that communication flow between you and the stakeholder, adapt it as time goes on and as you and the stakeholders' relationship develops.

It is possible that your own PMO has only a short period of time to demonstrate value, before it is carefully reviewed and its life expectancy challenged.

So the answer to 'what's in it for me?' can be 'my PMOs existence!'

The PMO Acid Test

What happens when you call up a project manager? Do you get straight through or do they adopt an avoidance strategy?

A call from any member of the PMO should be a welcome event and not something to hide from or fear.

31

2 What Makes a PMO Successful?

In this chapter we analyze what the key parties involved in the world think of PMOs in general and what makes some more successful than others. We hear from PMO leaders, PMO sponsors and PMO members; and assess what it is that they are all looking for in their PMO leaders.

VOICES, I'M HEARING VOICES

Let's reach outside our personal knowledge zone and conduct a 360-degree assessment.

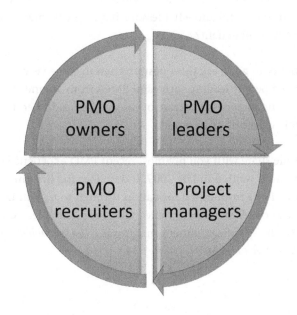

The 360 refers to the 360 degrees in a circle, with you (and me) as individuals figuratively in the centre of the circle. Feedback is provided by as many other interested stakeholders as possible in order to provide a balanced and informed view of the individual.

The results from the feedback will help you assess where you are doing things right and where you need to think about improving.

So within this particular 360 degrees I have, on your behalf, reached out to firstly, other PMO leaders, secondly all those project managers who work in the PMOs and then, the very employers that hand out those prime PMO leadership roles (see the figure on the previous page: the 360 degrees of PMO stakeholders). To this I have added some insight from the 'C' level executives who sponsor the whole PMO world.

> *Without initiative, leaders are simply workers in leadership positions.*
>
> Bo Bennett

THE VOICE OF THE PMO LEADERS

What do real PMO leaders say about their own PMOs? What has made them successful and what lessons have they learned from which we may all benefit?

Where better to go to ask this question than to some very experienced people leading successful PMOs from around the world. The following includes a mixture of case studies and interviews to give you insight into their world.

First, let me share with you my most recent PMO experience taken from an article written in late 2009. It describes the first three years of my own PMO from initial formation through to a point in time when it was closely reviewed, valued and – and I am pleased to say – kept, with the specific comment that it was, *'Too valuable to lose (and not too expensive to keep).'*

The work did not stop there and since this article was written the PMO has evolved into two PMOs, each with a closer focus on two geographical and business areas and with my initial PMO recruit now heading up that second PMO. We remain closely aligned in order to share our combined capabilities and experience.

Siemens PLM Software

The first commercial product developed by what is now known as Siemens PLM Software was called UNIAPT. Released in 1969 by a software company then called United Computing, UNIAPT was one of the world's first end-user CAM products. United Computing was founded in 1963 above a hair salon in Torrance, California, and went on to purchase the Automated Drafting and Machining (ADAM) software code from MGS in 1973. The code became a foundation for a product called UNI-GRAPHICS, later sold commercially as Unigraphics in 1975.

The following year, United Computing was acquired by the Aerospace company McDonnell Douglas, who created new CAD/CAM divisions, naming one the Unigraphics Group. Finally, in 1980, Unigraphics was released, marking the group's first true 3D modelling hardware and software offering.

Already home to McDonnell Douglas, the Unigraphics Group grew in St. Louis, Missouri, which became the new headquarters. In 1991, the McDonnell Douglas Systems Integration groups, including Unigraphics, were acquired by EDS, calling the new group EDS Unigraphics. Eventually, in 1997 EDS set up its Unigraphics division as a wholly owned subsidiary called Unigraphics Solutions. EDS took Unigraphics Solutions public while continuing to own majority controlling shares in Unigraphics. During this time, Unigraphics acquired a few companies itself including Engineering Animation, Inc., the former Ames, Iowa-based visualization company.

In 1999 the company acquired Applicon, a long-term player in the EDA field.

Unigraphics changed its name to UGS in 2001. Also that year, EDS repurchased all outstanding UGS stock, and acquired a UGS

35

competitor, SDRC. UGS and SDRC were merged into a single Line of Business (LOB) named EDS PLM Solutions. EDS sold off its EDS PLM Solutions business to the private equity group of Bain Capital, Silver Lake Partners, and Warburg Pincus in 2004. The company resumed operating under the UGS name following the private equity sale.

In 2005, UGS purchased Tecnomatix Technologies Ltd.

On January 24, 2007 the German electronics giant Siemens AG announced that they would acquire UGS for $3.5 billion. When the sale completed, UGS became part of Siemens Automation & Drives group as Siemens PLM Software.

Also in January 2007 the EMEA services executive within, the soon to be known as, Siemens PLM Software invested in a PMO led by Peter Taylor.

The leadership experience

'Too valuable to lose (and not too expensive to keep)' – this was the best summary made on the PMO after a review in mid-2009 and it is one that I was proud to receive on behalf of the PMO team.

As organizations tried to deal with the economic downturn, they all took a long hard look at the ROI of just about every endeavour – including the PMO.

At Siemens Product Lifecycle Management (PLM) Software, we believed our PMO for the Europe, Middle East and Africa (EMEA) region still continued to bring value both to the organization and our customers. Our PMO, to give an indication of scale, oversees 100+ project managers and 200 projects with a revenue flow of $350m per year.

But what was the general view of the PMOs?

Well, an ESI International survey of 60 UK executives conducted in November 2008 found that many PMOs were being challenged on a number of fronts, including:

- the PMO was often seen as an extension of administrative support, rather than a professional body with value-add skills;

- budget cuts necessitated cost justification, a difficulty for the usually non-revenue producing PMO;

- the PMO size and organizational set-up were viewed as counter to the time constraints under which project managers operate; and

- there was a lack of understanding of the business benefits of the PMO, especially among executive management.

Even in these challenging times, the PMO within Siemens PLM Software is deemed 'fit for purpose'. I believe it's because we have evolved to be seen as supportive of the organization as a whole and not grown to a size that outweighs our business benefit.

37

We are too valuable to lose and but equally important we are not too expensive to keep.

What is a PMO?

One definition is that a PMO is a group or department within a business, agency or enterprise that defines and maintains standards for project management within the organization. The primary goal of a PMO is to achieve benefits from standardizing and following project management policies, processes and methods. Over time, a PMO generally will become the source for guidance, documentation and metrics related to the practices involved in managing and implementing projects within the organization.

Summarizing this then a PMO should:

- ensure that all projects are aligned with the overall business strategy;

- highlight key project interdependencies and align releases across interdependent projects;

- assist in timely decision making on the overall control of projects;

- approve change requests of global relevance; and

- monitor and report projects.

The ESI survey found that the role of a PMO generally covered three approaches: supportive, controlling and directive, and with a reasonably even spread across the survey businesses across those three types – controlling being the slightly dominant one.

What is the role of the PMO?

© ESI International 2010. The complete report is available at www.esi-intl.co.uk/resource_centre/industry-reports/index.asp

In terms of what activities a PMO gets involved in, the survey identified a whole range across the 60 businesses that were interviewed.

What activities does your PMO get involved in?

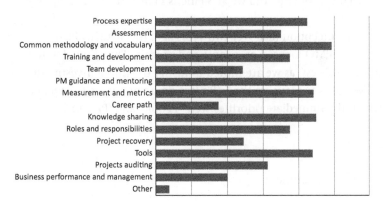

There was greater consistency between the factors that the PMOs felt contributed to their successes; with executive sponsorship coming out number one and alignment with the corporate goals being number two.

What do you see as the key factors for your PMO success?

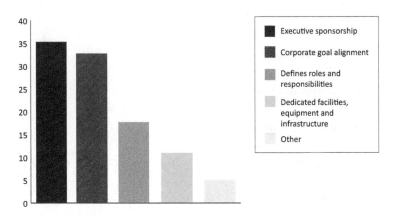

So what sort of PMO did we at Siemens PLM Software end up with?

From its inception just over two years ago, the Siemens PLM Software PMO focused on people and process. The original 'pitch' to the business, as we attempted to justify the initial investment in a PMO, was to focus on the 5 'P's (see figure on opposite page) of which the immediate priorities were 'People' and 'Process'.

People:

- recruitment

- profiles

- training

- induction

- certification

- assessment

- team building

Process:

- methodology

- certification programme

- quality assurance

- assessment

- authority

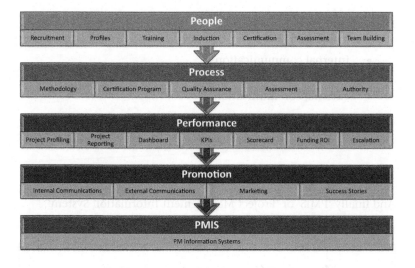

Over the last three years we have addressed all of the 'P's, with the Project Management Information System being the last to receive attention.

Thus we have added the three extra Ps of:

Performance:

- project profiling

- project reporting

- dashboard

- KPIs

- scorecard

- funding ROI

- escalation

Promotion:

- internal communications

- external communications

- marketing

- success stories

And finally 'PMIS' or 'Project Management Information System'.

> # You can't manage what you don't measure – so begin with some baselining activities to measure against

Once the PMO was established, a number of baselining activities were initiated:

- We completed a maturity assessment (Using Kerzner's 'KPMMM' process) in order to gain an objective view of the project management skill levels of our project managers as well the level of project management process adopted by our company.

- We undertook a survey to identify the project managers experiences, training, certification and current challenges.

- We promoted a 'bring out your dead' project amnesty in order to find the true 'health' of all of the current projects (or lack of health in some cases).

The survey of the project management community members and their local management initially identified three top issues:

1.   a lack of methodology or common process;

2.   a lack of skills or training; and/or

3.   poor resource management.

Consequently, the immediate focus was to improve these three critical gaps – the PMO supported the development of a standard global methodology and associated training of all project managers – a programme of training (in-house and through partners) and PMP certification began – and improvements in resource management (for example, creating a European-level escalation process of resource demands linking the field with product development – this was led by the PMO) commenced (these are now culminating in the implementation of a PMIS).

43

Year 1 of the PMO

Year 1 was all about creating a community and proving the value of membership of this community – both to the business and to the individuals involved.

In addition there was a high level of self-promotion and marketing – successes were shouted about and the PMO happily basked in reflected glory of successful projects and more direct glory for assisting some of the troubled projects.

Year 2

Year 2 involved focusing on improvements across the range of project management activities:

- project visibility – through the development of a project dashboard and regular reporting;

- Health Checks (PMO) – delivering quality audits for the largest projects and learning the common issues;

- retrospectives (PMO) – delivering project closure reviews (based on Norman L. Kerth's book on retrospectives) and gathering lessons learned;

- methodology training/adoption; and

- certification (PMP).

Year 3

Year 3 included local project management communities becoming self-sufficient:

- project methodology (each country had a local methodology champion trained in the method and skilled in training others); and

- Health Checks and Retrospectives (the PMO delivered training to local project managers).

In addition, the PMO became involved much earlier in the project life-cycle, through the pre-project initiation process. The PMO team took a role in reviewing and authorizing (or recommending improvements) in all significant projects before the customers received the draft statement of work.

A benefit and not a burden

By developing internal programmes aimed at addressing these issues, the PMO was seen as a supportive organization and not merely as administrative overhead. In some cases, we do take the lead on a few select projects (behaving in a directive manner). This way, the PMO both maintains real hands-on experience and also extends qualitative support and guidance to the local project managers.

Shortly after its formation the PMO extended its purview, from simply people and process, to performance and promotion. The move has ensured good communication of the PMO's benefits both to Siemens management across EMEA and to our customers. Delivering a regular newsletter, hosting knowledge-sharing sessions, showcasing project case studies, inputting updates to our methodology and never saying 'no' to requests for assistance have all helped put the PMO on everyone's radar as an organization that helps rather than hinders.

The PMO remains a small team of four, focused on supporting the larger project-organization of the business and involving a mix of all three PMO approaches: supportive, controlling and directive, as best suits the project needs.

Evolve your PMO to suit the business needs of your organization

---

45

And now, as promised, those other case studies and interviews involving PMO experts from around the world.

A big 'thank you' to all those who invested their personal time work to with me on the case studies and interviews.

The Doe Run Company

Based in St. Louis, The Doe Run Company is a privately held natural resources company and the largest integrated lead producer in the Western Hemisphere. Dedicated to environmentally responsible mineral and metal production, Doe Run operates the world's largest single-site lead recycling facility, located in Missouri.

Prior to 2006, The Doe Run Company had no formal project management in place. While project performance was not routinely tracked, there are examples of projects completing 100 to 200 per cent over schedule and budget. There was no formal training in project management processes for Doe Run personnel. Most projects were managed by external project managers with little Doe Run oversight. After years of projects being delivered significantly over schedule and over budget (and not delivering agreed-upon business objectives), ownership lost confidence in Doe Run's project management capabilities. As a result, every project estimated to cost over $10,000 required pre-approval from the Board of Directors.

In 2006, the company struggled with a large enterprise resource planning implementation which was led by a functional manager with no project management experience. Despite an initial resistance to 'adding bureaucracy', frustration drove company management to look for a better answer. On the recommendation of the CIO, the PMO was created in 2006.

The PMO was established with a decentralized structure and is staffed by one project manager and one business analyst. Engineers in each division serve as project managers but do not report directly to the PMO. While reporting to the CIO and funded within the IT budget, the PMO is responsible for providing mentoring and oversight to projects company-wide, including construction and engineering projects as well as corporate and IT projects. The PMO provides oversight to approximately 40 projects at any point in time with projects ranging in size from $10,000 to $150 million.

The primary goal of the PMO was to reduce surprises in projects through better planning, setting realistic expectations and improving the quality of information on projects.

The leadership experience

One of the first actions of the Doe Run PMO was to purchase a project management methodology designed for the mining vertical market and customize the methodology to meet specific Doe Run needs. The methodology was named the 'Project Delivery System' and provided a set of flexible processes, tools and templates that were designed to manage a project through its lifecycle. Project funding requests must include a description of the current problem or opportunity, alternatives that were evaluated, and a detailed description of the proposed solution. Guidelines are provided for making accurate cost and schedule estimates.

A key component of the Doe Run project management methodology is a gated process for approving projects. The methodology is flexible and the number of approval gates varies with the size and complexity of the project. In the past, significant expenditures would have been made on engineering before a request for funding was made for the entire project cost. Once such major expenditures were made, management was reluctant to cancel these projects in progress due to the 'sunk cost'. The goal of the gated approval process was to provide just enough information at each phase of the project to make a good business decision whether or not to fund the next phase of the project. As a result, several major projects have been cancelled in early stages of development, when it was determined capital expenditure requirements were too high for the potential benefit or that the project no longer fit with company strategy.

A critical new product development project was chosen as a pilot for the new methodology. Despite a lack of project management experience, the assigned project manager was willing to adhere to the new standard practices. The methodology proved a major help to the team as they considered alternatives for the project in regards to technology, location and production capacity. This initial success was communicated throughout the organization and the project manager served as cheerleader for the new process.

In establishing common project management processes, it was important that all stakeholders spoke a common language and used terms that business leaders could understand. Education on the project management methodology, best practices and terminology was provided through regularly scheduled training classes offered by the PMO.

Project sponsors throughout the organization attended a three-hour overview on the project sponsor role in project success. Guidelines were provided on what a project sponsor should expect from a project manager and tools such as standard status report formats and 'key questions to ask about the project' were provided to project sponsors. This training helped project sponsors become comfortable with their role in holding project managers responsible for project delivery.

A baseline measuring the impact of the PMO on project results was taken at the end of 2007 after new processes had been in place for one year. By the end of 2009, the percentage of projects meeting schedule objectives increased from the baseline of 25 per cent to 40 per cent and the percentage of projects meeting cost objectives increased from 71 per cent to 85 per cent. More importantly, the percentage of projects achieving stated business objectives dramatically increased from 62 per cent to 95 per cent.

Through the work of the PMO, confidence in the ability of Doe Run personnel to successfully deliver projects has increased to a level that the Board of Directors raised the dollar limit for requiring Board approvals from $10,000 to $500,000. Additionally, the average time for project funding approval has dropped from 98 days to an average of 22 days.

Top tips for would-be successful PMO leaders

To help ensure adoption of PMO best practices, tailor your PMO implementation to your organization. While the steps to implement a PMO may be common across different types and sizes of organizations, the way those steps are implemented should vary based on the organization's culture.

Tailor your PMO to your business needs

To help understand the organization's culture and method of doing business ask the following:

- What are the current 'pain points' of your organization in regards to project initiation, management and delivery?

- How can a PMO provide the most value to your organization?

- What techniques have worked when introducing other types of organizational changes to the organization? What techniques did not work?

Understand your organization's culture

Organize a team with representatives from key areas of the organization to help you answer these questions and determine the best fit and implementation strategy for the PMO. The team can help you identify those WIIFM ('what's in it for me') opportunities that will help drive PMO adoption and success. At Doe Run, a cross-functional team identified the major pain point as slow turnaround time for project funding approvals. The WIIFM for project managers was showing how improvements in project delivery would reduce turnaround time for project funding, enabling critical projects to be completed as needed to meet operational needs.

49

Tailoring a PMO implementation to the needs of your organization includes:

- Using a flexible project management methodology. The methodology must be flexible enough to provide an appropriate level of structure based on the size and complexity of the project without requiring unnecessary work. The Doe Run Project Delivery System includes a simple five question survey that calculates project complexity based on estimates of time, cost, technology and operational impact. The number of project approval gates required and the level of project management expertise needed vary based on complexity.

- Providing examples of what success looks like using examples from your own organization.

- Establishing a centralized or decentralized PMO structure to align with company organizational structure.

- Determining the role of the PMO (supportive, controlling or directive) based on organizational culture. At Doe Run, we anticipated it would be difficult to drive user adoption at a company which had used the same operational methods for over 140 years, so we selected a 'supportive' role for the PMO. Working side-by-side with operational managers with a 'we're here to help' attitude went much further at driving behaviour than a more controlling approach.

- Looking at the typical rate of organizational change when determining speed of implementation for the PMO.

Implementing a PMO is just like any other project. Create a project charter that outlines not only the mission and vision for the PMO, but also implementation steps to drive user adoption. Don't underestimate the time and effort required for organizational change. Project management processes only work if they are adopted by the people who should be using them.

Understand your organization's culture and way of doing business

Deal with 'what's in it for me'

Tailor the PMO

Treat it like a project

Reduce surprises!

Biography of author

Denise Callahan, PMP, is currently the manager of the PMO at The Doe Run Corporation, a major mineral and metals producer, headquartered in St. Louis, MO. Denise has over 20 years of experience managing IT projects and leading IT organizations and has successfully established PMOs at three major corporations.

The Doe Run PMO was a finalist for the 2010 PMO of the Year Award, sponsored by PM Solutions and the PMO Special Interest Group (PMOSIG) of the Project Management Institute (PMI®). Denise is an accomplished communicator and has spoken at international conferences on project management topics.

The leadership interview – a PMO with 'mana'

Chris Pope holds a Bachelor of Arts in Communication, Master of Arts in Theology, and has held a PMP certification since 2001. He has spent the past 15 years combining project management and business leadership expertise with a pragmatic approach to rescue projects and business units in crisis, manage complex enterprise-wide information technology projects and streamline business processes. He has worked in industries including airline, management consulting, local government, healthcare, telecom, Internet, and non-profit.

Chris grew up in the United States and resides in New Zealand. He currently manages a PMO and often speaks on various business leadership and project management topics. You can find him on LinkedIn.

Interview

Peter: Chris, perhaps you can start by explaining the term 'mana'?

Chris: Of course. In the New Zealand lexicon, 'mana' is a word that comes from the original inhabitants, the Maori. It refers to authority, influence, prestige or status. This is the substance of personal presence that is required to be leader that others will follow.

Peter: OK, so how does that link in with your PMO experience then?

Chris: Not too long ago, I had to set up a PMO with mana. It needed 'street cred' (a term from my native homeland – the United States) with the project management community, and strategic value with the senior management.

The challenge was made more difficult by the previous incarnation of a PMO. It was seen as bureaucratic and administrative. It was big on process, with enough templates to make any pedantic paper-lover giddy with excitement.

Peter: That doesn't sound like it would have been a great PMO under which to be a project manager?

Chris: Not at all. Unfortunately, the one-size-fits-all process was not a good fit at all! I am sure that the process, tools and templates would have gotten an 'A' from a business studies professor, but it got a resounding 'F' from the project managers and business managers who used it ... thus, two years prior to my arrival, the previous PMO was disbanded because it did not add any real value.

Peter: So how long after that did you get the challenge?

Chris: It was two years later, and here comes the 'new guy' with his American accent and singular mission – set up something that we just got rid of because it didn't work! Great. Let's see how long he lasts ...

Needless to say I had a challenge – I knew that a PMO could bring significant benefits to the organization (of course that is what the last guy said). I had to overcome the 'Ghost of PMOs Past', win over a sceptics who had 'heard it all before', and prove that a PMO could deliver benefits higher up the value chain than pushing unwanted paper through an unwanted process.

Peter: So what would recommend to other PMO leaders put in a similar position?

Chris: If you are ever in a situation where you need to (re)establish a PMO in an environment that questions whether the whole thing is worth doing, here is my advice.

Start with an audit and action plan

Start with an audit and action plan – this is true of any manager coming into a new role, but never more so than when you know that the department was underperforming and you need to establish why (and what should be done about it). In the interview for the role, I told my prospective boss, 'Give me one month to conduct a thorough audit of the organization's project delivery practices and develop my action plan.' I set this expectation with everyone I spoke with so that they all understood that I was on a one-month deadline, and no outputs or major decisions would be seen until after I had clearly identified the organization's needs and next steps.

Acknowledge the cynicism – I was upfront that I knew that the past PMO was not successful, they may have heard it all before and that they may have their doubts about whether or not the new PMO will be any different. However, give me a chance and judge me by the results you see in the coming months.

Use the quick wins to establish your credibility – make sure that your action plan has highly visible impacts that you can deliver quickly. This will go a long way to overcoming the initial cynicism of those who have 'seen it all before'. This initial delivery will establish your credibility as someone who does what they say and gets results. This proof that you get things done will help you get the buy-in that you will need to accomplish the longer-term changes.

Act like a business leader and not a project manager

Speak like a business leader – not a project manager. Your customer does not understand earned value; activity-based costing or the glories that are the PMBOK®! If they were as enamoured with the intricacies of project management as you are they would be a project manager. They do, however, understand things like, cost/benefit, prioritization, strategic objectives, efficiency and customer satisfaction. This is the language that you need to use when engaging them. When speaking to stakeholders, I focus on the outcomes of the project, how these address their pain points, what trade-offs are made if they promote this project over that one, and how the projects help them achieve their targets.

Be pragmatic! People are leery of new standards and processes unless they see a clear rationale and benefit to doing them. One of the things people want to know when you are looking at instituting new practices is that you will not waste their time with unnecessary work that does not add value. My mantra from day one was, 'If that activity (template, tool) is not adding value, why are you doing it?' A PMO manager who makes a stand that only activities that show tangible value to the organization or the project team will be supported is a relief to those who were previously burdened with unnecessary overhead.

Develop the new processes and tools with the people who will use them – it is always important to engage stakeholders when developing a solution. This is especially true when they were not happy with the last one. I made sure to involve the project managers when developing the project management practices, as well as the other stakeholders for revamping the governance processes.

Peter: Chris, excellent advice. Thank you.

Start with an audit and action plan

Acknowledge the cynicism

Go for quick wins

Act like a business leader

Be pragmatic

**Develop tools and processes
with the users**

ESPN

Founded by Bill Rasmussen and his son Scott Rasmussen, ESPN launched on September 7, 1979 under the direction of Chet Simmons, the network's president and CEO (and later the United States Football League's first commissioner). Getty Oil Company provided the funding to begin the new venture. Geoff Bray of New Britain, CT was chosen as the architect. George Bodenheimer is ESPN's current president, a position he has held since 1998.

ESPN's signature telecast, SportsCenter, debuted with the network and aired its 30,000th episode on February 11, 2007. ESPN broadcasts primarily from its studios in Bristol, Connecticut. The network also operates offices in New York City, Seattle, Washington, Charlotte and Los Angeles. The Los Angeles office, from which the late-night edition of SportsCenter is now broadcast, opened at LA Live in early 2009. The name of the sport company was lengthened to 'ESPN Inc.' in February 1985.

ESPN markets itself as 'The Worldwide Leader in Sports'. The slogan appears on nearly all company media.

Most programming on ESPN and its affiliated networks consists of live or tape-delayed sets of events and sports-related news programming (such as SportsCenter). The remainder includes sports-related talk shows.

On June 11, 2010, ESPN launched ESPN 3D, the first 3D TV channel in the US. The first programming in the format was the 2010 World Cup. ESPN states another 100 live events will be broadcast in 3D in the first year.

The leadership experience

Having started up a PMO in one large company, working in others and creating a global PMO Center of Excellence for yet other, I've seen my share of methodologies and processes – good and bad – and have learned what works and what doesn't.

When I joined ESPN in 2007 as a senior portfolio manager, the technology PMO had been in existence for about three years and they had implemented one of the most feature-rich portfolio management tools on the market. This violated one of my PMO best practices (although not mine to claim!); the focus of building a reputable and successful PMO should be on people, process then tools!

Focus on people

Focus on process

With a PMO staff of seven project managers and some basic methodology documentation, the application development organization the PMO supported was reluctant at best to adopt another organizations staff 'telling them what to do'. The progress since I started has been achieved by another simple PMO best practice – knowing your customer and providing superior customer service. The development organization manages a lot of work from application support and maintenance, to enhancements along with the PMO-led projects. Providing them with a process and tool to support all of their work, along with helping them get data set up in the tool has greatly improved our perceived value to the organization.

Top tips for would-be successful PMO leaders

Here are some more suggested best practices all wrapped around sports concepts to make them a little more fun (well I do work for ESPN after all).

Focus on the team
Let's start with the core of most sports, the team. On most projects, as with team sports, a well-functioning team is essential to success. It all starts with clear roles and responsibilities. This is where many organizations get some basic concepts confused. A role is not the same as a job or position. Roles are filled by staff with certain expertise and often the same person may fill multiple roles on a project team. Understanding the responsibilities of each role on the team allows the project manager to ensure the right resources are filling the right roles. Defining the core responsibilities for each role helps create a starting point for the team to work with. This brings me to the first key PMO best practice ... flexibility. It's rare that a project team would take a standard definition of roles and responsibilities and use it as is on a project. In some industries, such as construction and manufacturing, where projects are fairly standard and repeatable it's possible, but in most major corporations, and especially on IT software development projects, flexibility is the key.

You'll see this key concept of flexibility in other areas of this chapter, another way to think about it is to be *situational* – you need to be able to adapt and modify when needed to fit the type of project, the style of team and the culture of the organization. This includes the way you run the project – communications, meetings, project plan details and so on – along with the PMO standards, processes, methodology and templates, unless they are specifically required.

Guiding the team

In sports, with every team, there's a set of other people involved in helping the team perform whatever game they're playing. There are coaches, league officials, umpires and others that may be involved, some directing the overall league and schedule, others at each game to ensure the game is properly played.

The coach

The coach analogy brings up my second PMO best practice, identifying Subject Matter Experts (SMEs) to help project managers and teams. The project managers' skill set is extensive; consider the PMBOK® Knowledge Areas as a starter – you need to be good at integration, defining and controlling scope, managing time, estimating cost, ensuring quality, leading people, delivering communications, defining risks and understanding procurement. Most project managers have expertise in at least one area; communications, facilitation, work breakdown structure creation and so on. Identify your experts in the PMO or senior project managers with certain expertise in the organization. Utilizing them as coaches to other teams will not only help the project teams but gives the coaches a level of satisfaction assisting other teams.

The league officials

The 'league officials' who coordinate the entire operation are the senior managers who oversee the project portfolio and resources. Depending on the PMO structure in your organization, they could be acting as an enterprise PMO or you may have business unit PMOs that focus on a particular line of business. In any case, these managers work with the business and customers to identify and prioritize the work for the teams to execute and usually govern the portfolio of projects.

The umpire

Perhaps the least liked figure in sports, the umpire, is also perhaps the most important. Consider how a game would be played without an impartial participant to oversee and help ensure the proper outcome. The umpires in the project management world then, provide the governance necessary to ensure the project team is set up properly and heading for success. Typically acting on behalf of a PMO, and similar to the coaching model, the 'umpires' (or governators as we call them!) can be staff in the PMO or senior project managers providing oversight of their peers. The attitude and approach to governance is the key, they should work more like a good youth little league umpire; providing assistance to the players and teams by explaining what they did incorrectly and how to handle situations in the future rather than just telling them what they did wrong. In other words, they need to provide consulting and advice rather than just calling fouls and penalties.

Rules of the game

One of the least understood, but critical, part of any sport are the rules of the game. For project teams, like teams in any sport, the rules must be well known, easy to understand and use and help the team be successful. The *rules of the game* from the PMO include the processes, methodologies and templates that support the project teams. One of my favourite activities working in various PMOs was to challenge the methodologists and the quantity of process documentation. This is where my third PMO best practice comes in: keep it simple and make it usable. The *rules* should be about providing guidance and support to get you where you're going ... it shouldn't be hard.

Process guides

Process guides should recognize the different learning styles human have – some of us are textual, some graphical – I'd rather see a map then read turn by turn instructions, others need the text to know where they're going. When producing process guides, provide both a text summary of the process you're documenting along with a graphic that depicts the process (a picture paints a thousand words they say).

Next, recognize that most organizations have project managers with a wide range of experiences – some only need basic information to get started. Where should the project scope get documented? Others need more guidance to capture the components of the scope statement. Start your process guides at a high level and allow the user to drill into more details when needed.

User aids

The next facet of human nature to be aware of is that very few people look at documentation after they first read it – if that even happens! Just as few will access help functions – when's the last time you hit F1 for help? This is where a simple user aid can help the project managers and teams. User aids can be developed to support your tools, process or roles – keep them easy to read and limit to one page (or double sided if needed). I typically produce these aids on hard-card stock paper so team members can carry with them in their portfolios or use as *cube wallpaper* – they will get way more usage than any process manual ever written.

One example of a user aid I created helps teams by summarizing the scope–requirements–design steps into a one-page reference that business users and customers can relate to. I use this user aid, along with others that focus on roles and responsibilities, and use of our portfolio management tool as the core user aids for all project managers and teams.

Templates

Templates are another part of the rules and a tremendous area of opportunity for an effective PMO. Templates linked to your methodology and process should be designed to help the project teams, and not make it harder to get their work done.

Keeping the flexibility concept (my first PMO best practice) in mind when dealing with template use is critical. Since each project is potentially different with different approaches and deliverables, templates should have clear required versus optional sections. Also allow teams to combine documents when it makes sense and, within the document, include sections for each possible area of information needs to consider, but make sure the teams know they can be deleted or combined.

Grounds crew

My next PMO best practice is taken from many successful companies, but rarely seen in PMOs – that is operating in a customer service model. Providing service to your customers or project teams is analogous to the grounds crew seen at major sporting events. The grounds crew in sports, as in a PMO, work to *prepare the field* and provide support to the teams in order for them to have a successful game. Whenever possible, the PMO should be assisting the project manager and project team as well; setting up project information in the tracking tool and creating a document repository for the team to use are just a couple of examples of how a PMO can provide customer service.

The quarterback

The project manager serves as the final sports analogy as the quarterback of the team. They need to prepare for the *game*, making sure they know their *opponent*. They need to work with their team to lead them to victory – not be a coach on the sidelines – but should utilize the coaches when needed. Like a quarterback in the NFL, they need to *manage the clock*, making sure they keep the schedule and target in mind, taking a timeout when needed. Above all, utilizing proper risk management principles, they need to *anticipate the hits* to avoid taking a major loss.

My final PMO best practice ties back to a basic continuous process improvement concept: you can't improve what you can't measure. Getting the voice of the customer is critical in process improvement and the PMO should constantly be trying to improve and increase its value to the organization. They need to relate to their customers/users, involve them in decisions and communicate with them often.

A valuable tool I found to get the voice of the customer in order to help measure the effectiveness of the PMO, quantifying its value and defining areas of improvement, is a simple periodic customer survey. Use the survey to find out what's working, what can use improvement and collect any ideas or volunteers to help out. Make sure you communicate back to the survey participates with a summary of what you collected and what you plan to do about it. Keeping the survey questions similar year to year will help measure the effectiveness of changes made during the year, remember – you can't improve what you don't measure.

> # You can't improve what you don't measure
>
> # Keep it flexible
>
> # Aid but don't burden

Biography of author

With over 25 years of project management experience, Michael (Mike) Leser works to share best practices and solutions that improve PMOs and simplify the life of the project manager.

Mike has worked as project/programme manager at Aetna, led a PMO at CIGNA, formed a global PMO Center of Excellence at ING and is currently with ESPN as Senior Portfolio Manager.

He holds a Master of Science in Management of Information Systems from Rensselaer Polytechnic Institute, and a Bachelors degree in Business Administration and Computer Engineering from the University of Connecticut. Mike has also completed project manager training at IBM, the Project Management Certificate Program at Boston University, and was a part-time adjunct lecturer at Rensselaer Hartford. Mike is a PMI-certified Project Management Professional (PMP), and an Honored Fellow of the Life Office Management Association (LOMA).

The leadership interview – a PMO discussion

Gareth Byatt, Gary Hamilton and Jeff Hodgkinson are experienced PMO, programme and project managers who, starting in February 2010, agreed to collaborate on a three-year goal to write 50 articles (pro bono) for publication in any/all project management subject websites, newsletters and professional magazines/journals.

Their mission is to help proliferate good programme and project management practice, add value to the profession, and in earnest, hope readers gain benefit from their 60 years of combined experience.

As part of this commitment they agreed to a short interview on their thoughts on leading successful PMOs.

Interview

Peter: Guys, what is it, based on all of your personal experience, that you feel makes for a successful PMO?

Gareth: Peter, my first point of reference is this: what kind of PMO are we talking about? As we all know, PMOs come in many shapes and guises – and not all of them are called PMOs. Many organizations have groups or teams in their structure that perform the activities some of us call a PMO, they just happen to call them by different terms.

63

Most of us (certainly in the case of Gary, Jeff and myself, who are all PMO and programme managers) are familiar with the conceptual terms of different set ups of PMOs. For example, having an enterprise-level PMO at the top, coordinating overall activities, with portfolio management offices and programme management offices underneath to run portfolios and programmes of projects. And the traditional PMO, which may run projects, it is usually thought of as an office that provides guidance on the delivery methods to be used for running projects as well.

I have seen many examples of groups in organizations that are performing one or more of these functions, however they haven't bothered using the 'PMO' terminology – either as a conscious decision, or because they are just 'getting on with things' and do not pay attention to this type of terminology.

It is important in my opinion to set the foundation stones for success for any PMO by agreeing the overall purpose (and the vision, if you like) that the PMO is set up to achieve. This should be clearly defined at a couple of levels, and communicated to all stakeholders who are going to use the PMO to make sure the purpose and expectations are set.

Track the benefits – let your customers hold you to account

Just like with a project, I believe it is important to track the benefits of having a PMO or PMOs. One approach I like to take is to use a Balanced Scorecard approach, and as part of this to agree specific measures against which the PMO can be benchmarked. This can help to ensure the activities the PMO is supposed to perform are being 'held to account' by its customers.

For example, if you are running a programme management office with specific projects to deliver, I would suggest the following types of activities are important:

1. ensuring good practice programme and project execution;

2. providing strategic decision-making support;

3. governance;

4. performance monitoring and reporting; and

5. communications and resource management.

Peter: What are the dangers of failing to adhere to agreed roles and responsibilities do you think?

Gareth: Well, I've seen articles from practitioners that summarize the causes of potential failure quite well, for example:

1. unclear purpose;

2. inadequate buy-in to its existence;

3. perception of adding 'red tape' to delivery and increasing costs;

4.   negatively seen as 'the project management police';

5.   too academic and too removed from reality;

6.   veneer of participation, but no real 'teeth';

7.   incorrect or insufficient focus on the most important objectives; and

8.   it is hard to prove the value of the PMO.

Gary, what do you think?

Gary: I agree. PMOs should be viewed as an organization within an organization. In such, the PMO organization should have a charter, a strategic vision and a multigenerational plan.

65

An organization within an organization

Let's be clear: organizations without PMOs (or whatever term they operate under) cannot expect to go from zero to high-performing in this management area overnight, just as organizations don't go from start up to fortune 500 or FTSE 100 in a short period of time. They need to define what the 'gen-1 success' (perhaps the 'first phase', if you will) of the PMO will be.

Peter: So you see the PMO as a dynamic and evolving unit?

Gary: Absolutely. As the PMO matures it may change its responsibilities. The organization it is part of needs to have a strategic plan in place that evolves with the maturity of the PMO.

I also support the use of a Balanced Scorecard to define the delivery targets for a PMO; however, the metrics used on the specific Balanced Scorecard need to be evaluated and perhaps changed as the maturity of the PMO progresses. When PMOs are in their infancy you may want to measure common metrics such as 'on time' delivery whereas a mature enterprise-level PMO may measure other metrics. The metrics used on your Balanced Scorecard should reflect both the organizational strategic priorities as well as the maturity and function/responsibility of the PMO.

Peter: And Gary what are your personal thoughts regarding the dangers of failing to adhere to agreed roles and responsibilities?

Gary: I agree with the dangers Gareth has mentioned. In addition, I would expand on his point number 8 (proving the value of the PMO). Full agreement of roles and responsibilities is necessary to prove the value of the PMO; if these responsibilities are not in tandem with the delivery targets, there are risks to the PMO function as well as adoption of overall project management practices. If stakeholders are challenged to see the value of project, programme and portfolio management they will continually challenge the project, programme and portfolio managers who are in place to lead these initiatives, and ultimately it adds risk to the sustainability of the PMO that they work for (and probably report to).

Peter: Jeff, your thoughts?

C-level support is critical

Jeff: I tend to look at things from both points of view and therefore let's talk about what makes an unsuccessful PMO. Many of your readers can doubtless provide personal or observed examples but unsuccessful PMOs will most likely fall short in the following areas.

1.   You have to have senior management (C-level) executives' buy-in and understand what a PMO is along with the structure and benefits. They need to give probably a year to get a new PMO staffed and infrastructure set up along with the organizational culture change with the customers and stakeholders both internal (to the organization or company) and then external (to other company departments or your customers).

2.   You need a strong experienced leader to run a PMO. This person needs to be a manager and communicator. In this case prior experience as a project or programme manager is extremely helpful but not necessarily critical. A PMO manager with good people skills, strategic vision and business acumen can manage the department and ensure to hire or recruit strong experienced and credentialed programme/project practitioners to support all the requirements such as metrics, procedures, tools, central repository, work flow and processes. They must also be committed to a few years (at least two) to be in the position to benchmark and manage the change (year 1) and then optimize it (year 2) before it can be considered 'established' and then be a sustainable organization.

3.   The process of initiating a PMO must be considered a 'project in itself' from the point of initial approval through to when a year's worth of metrics (from initial benchmarking and problem documentation) are gathered. The overall performance deltas that the PMO provided to the organization/company (ROI for people, equipment and tools) should be factored in.

So if these three items of long-term senior management support and funding, having a strong PMO leader and approaching the set up of a PMO are in place, it stands a better chance of success for the long run. Without these three firmly in place long-term PMO success will likely be marginal at best.

Know what your PMO is about and therefore what it should focus on

A PMO is critical for a high-performing project business

Executive sponsorship is key

A strong leader of the PMO is essential

Peter: Gareth, Gary and Jeff great insight. Thank you.

PMO Leaders' Checklist

Status	PMO Leaders said:
	One size doesn't fit all, flexibility is key
	Balance well between people and process
	Never be afraid to promote your PMO and your projects
	Act like a business leader but have a continued passion for projects
	Track the benefits of what you are doing
	And be a strong leader

This is what the PMO leaders have told us is important.

Think about your PMO and your leadership style and skills – how do you score against these key points?

Leadership does not depend on being right.

Ivan Illich

THE VOICE OF THE PROJECT MANAGERS

All of these stories offer useful insight into what makes for a successful PMO but what do those who have experienced life before and, now during, the existence of a PMO feel?

What is the experience of the project managers under the guidance of the PMO? Has life improved or not? And what is still left to be done as far as they are concerned in order for their PMO to be considered totally successful?

I conducted a survey using Survey Monkey[1] and 822 respondents supplied their opinions and views and comments.

This survey represents the 'voice of the project managers', some of whom may be in your organization and served by your own PMO.

The survey[2]

It was important first to get some understanding of the survey audience so I began with a few positioning questions.

How long have you been part of a PMO?		
Answer Options	Response Percent	Response Count
Less than 1 year	18.9%	154
1 to 3 years	26.2%	213
Greater than 3 years	54.9%	446
answered question		813
skipped question		9

How long have you been part of a PMO?

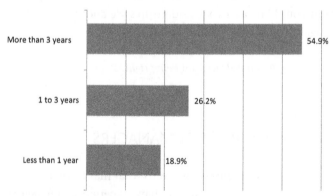

1 Survey Monkey has a single purpose: to enable anyone to create professional online surveys quickly and easily.
2 Further survey analysis can be found in the Appendices.

Question: How long have you been part of a PMO?

Comment: 81 per cent had been part of a PMO for more than a year which suggested some degree of maturity and therefore experience; increasing the credibility of the subsequent feedback.

I then asked about the roles.

What is your role within the PMO?		
Answer Options	Response Percent	Response Count
Head of PMO	27.0%	220
Programme manager	18.3%	149
Project manager	38.1%	310
Project office administrator	4.3%	35
Other	12.3%	100
answered question		814
skipped question		8

What is your role within the PMO?

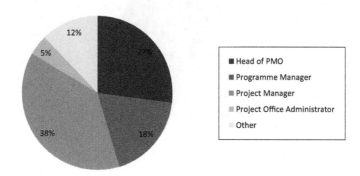

■ Head of PMO
■ Programme Manager
■ Project Manager
■ Project Office Administrator
　 Other

Question: What is your role within the PMO?

Comment: 73 per cent of respondents work with or within the PMO, rather than leading it, which again is what I was looking for in order to gain a feeling for the experience of PMO members, the project managers, the administrators and the programme managers, rather than the current PMO leaders.

Let's now look at the reach of the PMO's work – many PMO books speak only to PMOs that oversee internal projects but I particularly wanted to gather responses covering as wide a range of PMO activities as possible.

Is the PMO for which you work focused on:		
Answer Options	Response Percent	Response Count
Internal projects	43%	367
External projects	18%	155
Both	39%	334
answered question		814
skipped question		8

Is the PMO for which you work focused on:

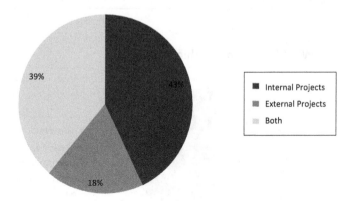

Question: What is the PMO for which you work focused on?

Comment: Only 43 per cent of the PMOs questioned address purely internal projects, 57 per cent cover external or a mixture; a good balance.

Now look at the 'before and after' effect.

Was the PMO created before or after your organization had a project management team?		
Answer Options	Response Percent	Response Count
Before	22.3%	152
After	77.7%	530
answered question		682
skipped question		140

Was the PMO created before or after your organization had a project management team?

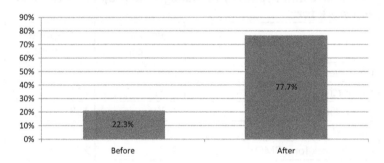

Question: Was the PMO created before or after your organization had a project management team?

Comment: As many as 78 per cent had experienced life in project management in their organizations before the creation of a PMO so the majority could speak to the 'before' experiences and compare these to the 'after' experiences. Another factor that brings value to the survey.

We identified three styles of PMO in earlier chapters:

1. The supportive-style PMO provides support in the form of on-demand expertise, templates, best practices, access to information and expertise on other projects.

2. The controlling-style PMO works in organizations where there is a desire to control project activities, processes, procedures and documentation.

3. A directive-style PMO moves beyond controlling and directly manages projects by providing the project management experience and resources.

Which of these styles did our survey contributors work under?

A supportive PMO generally provides support in the form of on-demand expertise, templates, best practices, access to information and expertise on other projects, and the like. A controlling PMO has the desire to guide the processes, procedures, documentation and so on towards a standard or standards. A directive PMO goes beyond control and actually 'takes over' projects by providing the project management experience and resources to manage the project. Is the PMO you work for:		
Answer Options	Response Percent	Response Count
Directive	18%	135
Supportive	31%	231
Controlling	21%	158
Blended	26%	198
I don't work for a PMO	4%	27
answered question		704
skipped question		204

Style of PMO

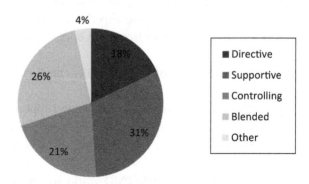

Question: What is the style of your PMO?

Comment: Interestingly 26 per cent work in a blended PMO – a PMO that combines elements of the supportive, controlling and directive approaches depending upon the situation and the need.

Directive was the least popular with 18 per cent and supportive the most popular with 31 per cent. Assuming that the blended PMO are also involved in supportive work then this suggests that 57 per cent of PMOs operate some form of supportive platform for their project managers.

But what about the project managers themselves?

I asked a number of questions to assess the experiences that they might have gone through, including questions about:

- support

- training

- career

- process

- project quality

- project success

- personal satisfaction

In each case I asked the respondents to compare and rate their experience before and after the implementation of the PMO.

How do you feel as a project manager working under a PMO – looking at the following aspects rate your current experience against the time when there was no PMO

Answer Options	Much improved	Better	No change	Worse	Much worse	I have always worked in the PMO	Response Count
Support	155	332	93	18	5	58	661
Training	88	278	212	26	4	54	662
Career	60	206	306	22	8	55	657
Process	158	348	62	29	10	53	660
Project quality	118	320	157	9	5	54	663
Project success	107	315	169	11	5	54	661
Personal satisfaction	91	297	160	39	17	54	658
answered question							665
skipped question							157

How have things changed since the advent of your PMO?

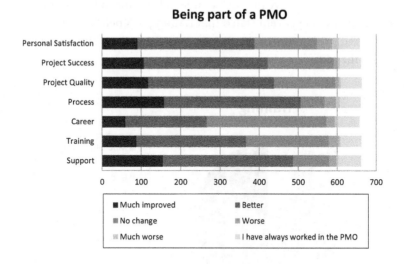

Being part of a PMO

Support

From the simple perspective of 'I feel better supported now I am part of a PMO' it seems that a PMO offers a huge benefit, with 73 per cent of respondents declaring that life is better or much improved now that they are part of a PMO. Add in the 'no change so it hasn't got any worse' and the figure rises to 87 per cent.

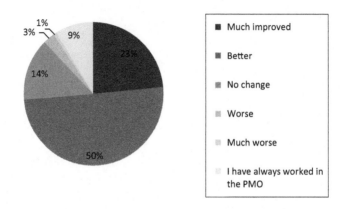

Support

Training

Training seems to have improved under a PMO too, although to a lesser extent. 55 per cent stated that training was better or much improved, with a further 32 per cent suggesting that things were just about the same.

Training

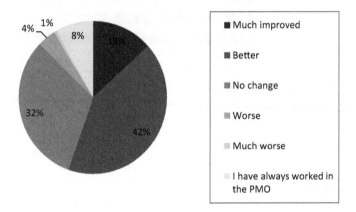

Career

On the career front, only 40 per cent felt that the clarity of career and potential to progress had improved within the PMO. 47 per cent had not yet seen any evidence that being part of a PMO aided such career advancement.

Career

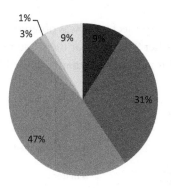

- Much improved
- Better
- No change
- Worse
- Much worse
- I have always worked in the PMO

Process

77 per cent of respondents had noticed (and perhaps benefited from) an improvement in process – definition and adherence – through the work of the PMO. Only 9 per cent had yet to see any form of process improvement.

Process

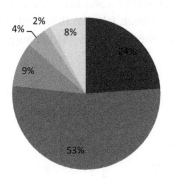

- Much improved
- Better
- No change
- Worse
- Much worse
- I have always worked in the PMO

Project quality

The improvement in the quality of project work was observed and reported by 66 per cent but a further 24% felt that there had not been any such improvement so far, through the governance of the PMO.

Project quality

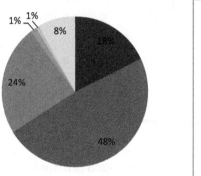

Project success

And as far as project success was concerned, 16 per cent felt that it was much improved and 48 per cent that is was better than during the pre-PMO existence. A quarter though felt that there had been no improvement (or decline either) – the situation was unchanged.

Project success

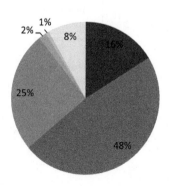

Personal satisfaction

Perhaps most pleasing, is to see that 59 per cent of PMO members felt that their personal satisfaction had improved under the wing of a PMO.

Personal satisfaction

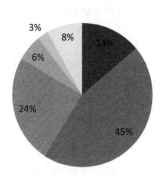

■ Much improved

■ Better

■ No change

■ Worse

■ Much worse

■ I have always worked in the PMO

81

Notes

Eight per cent of the people who took the survey had always worked under a PMO and therefore cast no view as to whether any of the above had improved or declined under a PMO. Between 3 per cent and 9 per cent felt that things had become worse or much worse through being part of a PMO, with the lowest statistics in the areas of project success and project quality and the highest in that of personal satisfaction.

Analysis

From the business point of view, I conclude that PMOs are successful given the significant number of respondents who indicate that projects are more successful and with a higher quality level (90 per cent stated that project quality was improved, or at least no worse, and 89 per cent declared the same for project success).

Behind this support for the PMO as a unit then support for the PMO members would also be critical, and we can see that through the 87 per cent approval rating for the PMO.

A lower number of respondents indicated an improvement in training under the PMO. It is not possible through this survey to understand if this is as a result of a lack of effective overall training framework and opportunity or because of specific training gaps. Nevertheless greater than half felt that training was better under the PMO.

More of a concern should be the consideration of success of the PMO from the project managers' point of view. The personal satisfaction rating is lower than I am sure all PMO leaders would wish. Similarly career opportunity improvement is also well below 50 per cent.

Of course, whilst it is true that you can't please all the people all of the time, PMO leaders must understand more why those 2 to 9 per cent felt that things had become worse or much worse through being part of a PMO. These negative responses may not apply to your own PMO but, if you want to be successful, beware of ignoring negative feedback; it is important to take a balanced view.

The project managers speak

Useful as such statistics are, the real mood of PMO team members can be gauged through their qualitative comments. I asked two specific questions as part of the survey:

Firstly: 'Since your organization has had a PMO in place what is the general view of the success of the PMO?'

And secondly: 'What do you feel are the most important aspects of being a successful leader of a PMO?'

Has your PMO been a success?

Remember that, overall, the survey respondents felt that the PMO they were working with had been a good thing and was seen as generally a success.

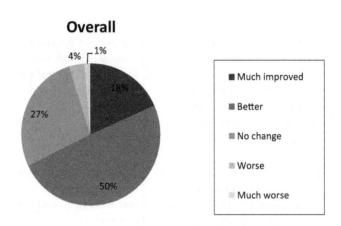

Overall

- Much improved
- Better
- No change
- Worse
- Much worse

Overall, have things improved or got worse since the PMO?

Only 5 per cent of those who had experienced life inside and outside a PMO felt that life had generally got worse (or much worse) so the vast majority felt that either there was status quo or indeed matters had improved.

But there was a good deal of comment left so let's look at this in three areas:

1.   The 'good': that is the PMO has demonstrated a positive effect on the business and projects.

2.   The 'bad': there are still lessons to be learned and improvements to be made.

3.   The 'ugly': where clearly the PMO has met with some failure.

The good

I like to start on a positive note and here is no exception.

You said your PMO had 'brought order to chaos'	Excellent testaments to the value of the PMO
And had delivered a platform for 'repeatable project success'	
You also said your PMO was 'very successful'. The organization has experienced the difference between PMO-led/PMO-supported projects and projects that went on their own – and it now looks to and expects that for project success, the PMO will be involved	It is clear in the survey results that the majority of people had experienced life before a PMO and life after a PMO with that 'life after' generally being a better life
The PMO was a 'good success, it has straightened out our project output quality and increased the range of services we can provide'	Therefore not just an improvement from 'life before' but an incremental improvement in capability moving forward
A great comment at the executive level was that 'the PMO brings decision support information to the decision makers'	An open visibility of projects proposed, in progress and delivered is essential to any business. You can't manage what you don't measure after all
'The portfolio management office has received strong support from the executive, who have commented that they have greater visibility and confidence in the quality and results achieved by the programmes and projects within the portfolio'	All very positive comments demonstrating that the executive support is in place and that the PMO has benefited the projects and the business
Linked to this you said, 'there's been a better level of metrics available for projects by ensuring that a Plan of Intent and Record are maintained'	
And, 'the general view of the success is positive. Since the forming of a PMO we've seen a reduction, almost elimination of "stealth" projects by other teams in the organization because they see the value of using project managers from the PMO who are trained and experienced professional project managers'	

'PMO standardizes project delivery and end results. It is possible to improve the process of each project because of the lessons learned'	So from a projects perspective a PMO sets the right standards and provides a basis to learn and improve
'The PMO has taken the pain away from the project managers and provides them with support on project control processes and timely management information that enables the project managers to put things right before they become massive issues. All of this enables the projects to better achieve on time and on budget delivery'	An excellent recommendation
And finally on the 'good news' front: 'a value added service'	In summary, a very positive image and reputation in the business, what we should all aim for with our PMOs
With the PMO being 'well received. We are sought out to manage projects'	

The bad

So there we have the 'good' but it wasn't all good, remember a reasonable percentage declared that there had been no change for the better under a PMO, as compared to before a PMO existed. And another group actually felt that matters had degraded since a PMO had been in place.

So what were the comments that the contributors to the survey stated?

One comment stated the experience under a PMO being 'not very good – not providing much value beyond trying to control process'	It appears that the 'bad' can be placed generally in to three categories. Firstly where the PMO is purely seen as a controlling body adding no additional value
And another declared the PMO was 'seen by some as an admin overhead and overly bureaucratic'	
'Our PMO is not flexible. Small and medium-sized programmes are overwhelmed with PMO processes intended for very large programmes/ projects'	Secondly where the PMO is inflexible and operates a 'one-size-fits-all' model for the processes

One person suggested their PMO's success was 'limited. They mostly collect information from the projects and consolidate reports for the big boss. They attempt to "improve" projects by raising the bar but it is only for their reporting. Despite requests, they've not done anything to assist'	The third category was a complaint that the PMO was merely focused on measurement. So here the PMO was clearly derailed from its initial objectives
And another said, 'at the time I set the PMO up it was meant to support project managers. It became a statistics engine for senior management'	
One final comment raised a concern over leadership, 'the management in charge of the PMO are highly experienced operational managers, each with a significant and solid track record. Unfortunately that expertise does not translate into projects where the deadlines, delivery management and interaction between different role-players are significantly more acute than in operational management'	And then there was the challenge of being led by someone who just doesn't understand projects
There was also a theme of concern around the fact that for the PMO members the PMO had only delivered 'extra work'	Presumably without them seeing any personal return on that additional investment from the individual project managers
Comments such as 'about 50 per cent of the organization feels it is successful and the other wants it dismantled'	This is all about the challenges of getting a PMO accepted and respected inside an organization. It points to a clear need to market and promote our PMOs in order to be seen as a success and a useful 'go to' resource for the business
And 'difficult to establish perception of the PMO's impact on project performance'	

So plenty of challenges there.

And the ugly

And now finally to the 'ugly' comments, the ones that show that in these particular PMOs all is really not well at all.

The business reaction to the PMO had been 'not at all positive'. The function has been axed twice resulting in project managers reporting into other managers in the IT department	Rather a desperate sounding response. Clearly this PMO had not been successful and the resulting sad state of affairs must have been incredibly destabling to all involved and cannot have improved project success in any way, in fact it would most likely lead to less successful projects led by distressed and unengaged project managers
One person declared that 'recent changes in PMO management have radically changed both the direction/function of the PMO and the perception of its success. It has moved from being supportive to more controlling and has if anything become a glorified management information shop. This is not what the project managers want nor is it really helping the organization deliver successful projects'	Here matters in this PMO had moved from a positive position to one of increased distrust resulting in negativity and reduced commitment to the PMO work
as 'at the time I set the PMO up it was meant to support project managers. It became a statistics engine for senior management'	Again, as in the 'bad' section, the concern that the PMO was not about project managers but more about measurement and the executive can clearly be felt
And finally a cry that the PMO experience was 'not good'	Perhaps here the 'one-size-fits-all' approach was attempted (and was shown to fail)
Together with 'projects have stalled because trying to fit them all into a single template rather than a framework. Essentially the PMO is now a bottleneck'	

So whilst there is an acceptance of the value of a PMO generally, some people in some organizations are still having a bad experience as their PMOs are either moving away from the initial plan or have become too focused in specific areas of what should be a very wide remit.

And the other

One of the most intriguing comments left against the question 'Since your organization has had a PMO in place what is the general view of the success of the PMO?' was just a simple 'sexy'. Whoever left that comment please do make contact with me so that I can learn just how to make a PMO that attractive (I am sure many of the readers would love to learn more about that)!

That could just be a whole new book, all on its own.

What makes a good PMO leader?

Through the voice of the project managers we know what makes for a successful PMO (and conversely what contributes towards creating a bad PMO), but what do the same audience feel that a good PMO leader should know and how should he or she act to make sure they deliver what the business needs? I have extracted quotations from the feedback and tried to cluster those that seem similar.

Let's start with the big picture. PMO leaders, good PMO leaders, successful PMO leaders should be *passionate about project management.*

> # Be passionate about projects and project management but act like a business leader

---

We have seen the concern about PMOs being led by operational managers who do not understand the (strange) ways of us project folk and that there is a critical need for a PMO to be led by someone who 'knows projects'. Perhaps in time the PMO might become a business unit that future CEOs and CIOs move through in order to gain a full appreciation of the businesses that they will one day lead, but for now, perhaps because the PMO is too new and too evolving in its nature, an experienced project person is best suited to the leadership role.

The next comment I really liked was the suggestion *'need to keep it simple'*. The ability to lead and communicate the PMO strategy in simple uncluttered non-complex ways to the PMO members and the external stakeholders seems like a good idea to me.

In addition, and according to the survey, the PMO leader should be 'diplomatic' and 'pragmatic' as well as being *capable of making tough choices*; in other words, decisive.

Be decisive

This is closely followed by the preference for PMO leaders who 'are great communicators', have 'the human touch' and 'are extremely well organized'.

Throw in 'stakeholder management' along with specific suggestions such as 'knowing the key executives and key processes' and 'the ability to influence key decision makers within the organization' as well as 'lead by example' and we are getting closer to the perfect PMO leader.

We also had comments such as 'being proactive' and having 'a broad understanding of project management, not just one method' to add to the existing list of skills.

Perhaps the best summary was provided by the project manager who said the head of a PMO needs to 'to be a nurse, a psychologist and a fire fighter all at the same time'.

What else?

Being a 'good marketing person' was key for securing support; hard to lead what you don't agree with for sure. 'Functioning as a change agent' suggests the importance of an appreciation of and understanding for change management at an organizational level. Finally, there was the need to be 'open minded and not doing process for process sake'. As well as the request 'to be tolerant in that not all projects fit the same box'.

All in all plenty of varied guidance from the project managers for what skills the PMO leaders should have under their belt.

I was particularly struck by the 'big picture' feedback:

- 'Be able to put PMO on the map and make it a respected part of the organization.'

- 'Have a clear vision of what it looks and feels like "when you get there", that is, reach a point of success.'

- 'Be consistent in approach and ensure the PMO is seen as an organization there to assist all.'

- 'Be able to understand the bigger picture and realise the PMO functions are only part of the story.'

Plenty of great feedback and a lot to take on board. To summarize, what were the most commented on or most often suggested skills for a good and successful PMO leader?

Top of the pops

The top three, as voted for by all of those PMO members were:

1. communication

2. people skills

3. project understanding

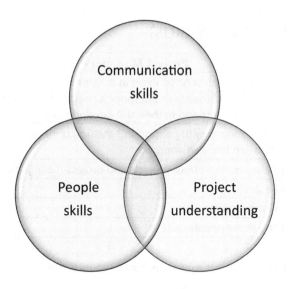

Top PMO leadership skills, in ranked order, were communication, people skills and project understanding, in other words being supportive of projects and project management.

Understandably in project work, in fact in any collaborative work, communication is rated highly. Perhaps those respondents who were less sanguine about their experience of working with a PMO may have experienced poor communication in terms of what the PMOs strategy is and future direction?

People skills is rated second and clearly being a leader does require you to gather support for what you, and the PMO, are trying to achieve; both for the business and for the project managers.

Finally, as a PMO leader you do need to understand the project-based world. Respondents made a number of comments about PMO leaders who, successful as they had been in operational management roles, were struggling to lead their PMO, for want of a good understanding of projects and project management.

PMO LEADERS' CHECKLIST

Status	Project Managers said:
	PMO is mostly a good thing as it helps bring order to their projects and their lives but more is needed to engage them in their careers and in their skill development
	Don't swamp with process and method unnecessarily get the right blended approach
	Be supportive about projects and project management
	Be decisive
	Communicate well
	Use those people skills

This is what the project managers have told us is important.

92

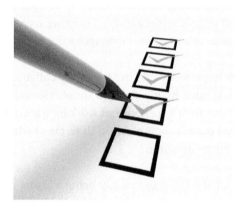

Think about your PMO and your leadership style and skills – how do you score against these key points?

> *Management is doing things right; leadership is doing the right things.*
>
> Peter Drucker

THE VOICE OF THE MARKET

What are recruiters and would-be PMO led companies asking that their new business leaders have on their resume?

As we have already heard the views of PMO leaders themselves and compared these to the views of the project managers, let's round this off with a view of what the 'market' is asking for; what the companies that are already won over to the value of a PMO are expecting from candidates.

I analyzed 100 advertisements for PMO leaders/heads/directors/ vice presidents across Europe and the Americas and Asia and this is essentially what I found.

PMO head – job advertisments

Skill	Asia	USA	Europe	Total
	10	**35**	**55**	**100**
Method/methodology	1	4	11	16
Negotiation skills	2	8	17	27
Change management/ agent of change	4	7	17	28
Self-managing/organized	4	10	22	36
Communication skills	6	13	28	47
Previous PMO experience	3	2	15	20
Risk management capability	2	5	10	17
Quality assurance	0	1	5	6
Strategically competent	2	8	8	18
Stakeholder management skills	1	6	16	23
Project management experience	4	2	6	12
	29	66	155	250

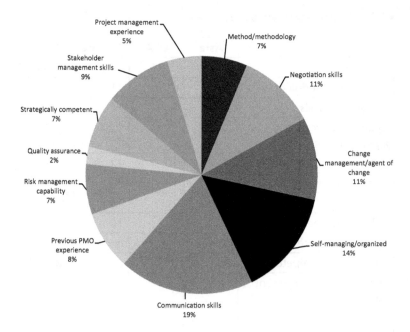

Recruitment Skills: PMO Leaders

Recruitment Skills: PMO Leaders (World)

Disclaimer: Now since job advertisements use a whole range of formats and structure and language and terminology, the above chart reflects my personal 'translation' of what recruiters were seeking from their PMO heads, leaders, directors, senior directors, vice presidents and managers.

Starting from the bottom of the graph:

- Method/methodology:

  - having a methodological background or experience, having developed a methodology, having used a standard methodology.

- Negotiation skills:

  - whether negotiating with the business, with customers, with PMO members, and with project champions.

- Change management/agent of change:

  - the ability to lead through change and to deal with change pressures.

- Self-managing/organized:

  - the expectation that a successful candidate would take up the reins of the job and self-manage themselves, act independently and be well organized, and bring organization to the projects themselves.

- Communication skills:

  - the capability to communicate the role and purpose of the PMO to all stakeholders and to communicate effectively.

- Previous PMO experience:

  - having either led or been part of a PMO previously.

- Risk management capability:

  - understanding risk, planning to handle risk, taking risks and dealing with risk.

- Quality assurance:

  - bringing a quality control discipline to proceedings, within and around a project.

- Strategically competent:

  - strategic competence involves understanding how individuals, teams and important stakeholders (as well as the business itself) all develop strategy and then responding to this by evolving the PMO accordingly. By default believing the PMO is not a fixed in time unit.

- Stakeholder management skills:

  - understanding the importance of positively engaging all of the stakeholders surrounding and benefitting from and contributing to the project activities.

- Project management experience:

  - having had project management practical experience over a number of years and qualified in some way. Interestingly none asked for programme or portfolio experience.

And so we see the clear requirement for four skill sets:

1. communication skills;

2. self-managing capability;

3. being an agent of change; and

4. having the skills of negotiation.

Interestingly previous project or PMO experience ranked only sixth on the list. It may have been that recruiters assumed previous experience, based on the other required skills.

Strategy came in only at joint seventh place.

There were some geographical variances which might be useful to at least be aware of as well:

Asia	First	Communication skills
	Joint Second	Self-management skills
		Change management skills
		Project management experience
	With previous PMO experience coming fifth and project management experience, as we can see, coming joint second.	

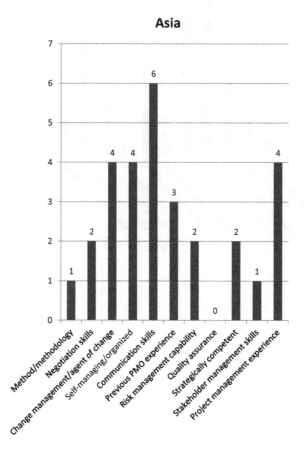

Asia

USA	First	Communication skills
	Second	Self-management skills
	Joint Third	Negotiation skills
		Strategy skills
	With previous PMO experience and project management experience coming joint ninth.	

USA

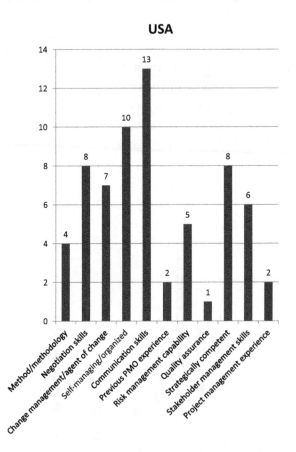

Europe	First	Communication skills
	Second	Self-management skills
	Third	Change management skills
	Fourth	Negotiation skills
	With previous PMO experience coming sixth and project management experience coming tenth.	

Europe

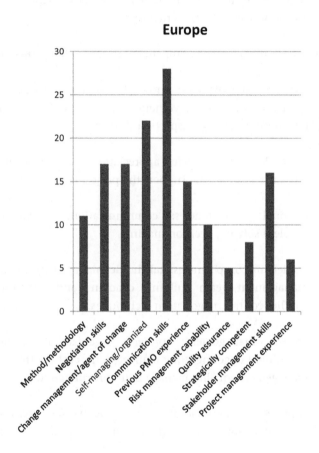

Missing or presumed there?

I think that there is one presumption that it is fair to make and that is all of the above requirements listed for competent PMO leadership assume that the candidates had a strong project management competency.

Asia aside (with project management skills coming in second on the 'want' list) the 'we need you to understand the basics of project management theory' and 'we want you to have a practical background based on personal experience' must be presumed.

It seems that around the world, as companies seek new PMO leaders, they are placing more emphasis on other skills and experience beyond those of project management basics.

A typical Project Management Competency Framework will include:

- Business competencies: knowledge of the business and business systems, governance and compliance and regulatory rules, legal aspects and so on.

- Technology competencies: appreciation and knowledge of any such systems that support the project delivery process.

- Personal competencies: communication, networking, problem solving, decision making.

- Leadership competencies: stakeholder management, change management, team building, coaching and mentoring, conflict control, negotiation techniques.

- Project management: project organization, project planning, budgeting, time management, cost control, risk management, quality management, procurement.

An effective project manager should score well across these areas and a future PMO leader should score highly in all of them.

PMO Leaders' Checklist

Status	Managers of PMO Leaders said:
	Communicate well
	Negotiate fairly and strongly
	Be an agent of change
	Demonstrate self-managing capability
	Believe in the business and the projects
	And know the project world

This is what the managers of PMO leaders have told us is important.

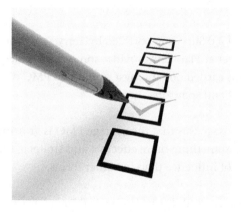

Think about your PMO and your leadership style and skills – how do you score against these key points?

> *The very essence of leadership is that you have to have vision. You can't blow an uncertain trumpet.*
>
> Theodore M. Hesburgh

THE 'C'-LEVEL VOICE

It is much harder to come by a top executive view of PMOs. They don't tend to respond to surveys or LinkedIn discussions. And yet they can choose either to support, ignore or remove a PMO within their business. Their sponsorship is absolutely critical.

One viewpoint at this level is that we can see an increase in PMO existence, maturity and longevity. That is to say that organizations are accepting the PMO as a key business unit and are connecting that unit to business strategy, which in turn makes the PMO's planning horizon a long-term affair. And with the investment in such PMOs it is attracting the best project personnel, which aids its maturity and capability.

The 2008 PMO 2.0 Survey Report[3] led by Terry Doerscher, Chief Process Architect at Planview provides some useful C-level insights. The survey was carried out amongst over 1,000 PMO directors, managers, staff and sponsors.

The overall message was that the average PMO is growing and changing into something more effective and strategic that has a broader range of influence than in earlier forms.

> *The survey yielded a wide range of line of reporting for the PMO … which further reflects the diversity of PMOs participating … Collectively, over half of the PMOs participating in the survey (55 per cent) report to a C-level executive (CIO/CTO included), while another 10 per cent answer directly to a vice president.*

> *While one might suspect that PMOs reporting to higher levels of the organization may tend to focus more exclusively on capital projects, the general span of PMO functions (Projects Only, All Planned Work, or Planned*

---

3   2008 PMO 2.0 Survey Report - The Continued Evolution of the Project, Program and Portfolio Management Office (PMO) Terry Doerscher, Chief Process Architect, Planview Inc. See http://www.planview.com/docs/Planview-2008-PMO-2.0-Survey-Report.pdf.

> *Work and Operations) was uniformly distributed regardless*
> *of the PMO line of reporting.*
> Terry Doerscher, Chief Process Architect, Planview Inc.

There was a particularly useful comment in the introduction:

'The State of the PMO 2010'[4] report by PM Solutions stated: 'The upward trend is unmistakable, both in sheer numbers of PMOs and in the rising organizational clout.'

Other key points from the survey revealed that:

- 64 per cent of the PMOs advise their executives;

- 62 per cent of the PMOs participate in some form of strategic planning;

- and nearly 60 per cent of PMO directors/leaders report in to the level of executive vice president or above.

All of which supports the impression of a growing and impressive 'C'-level support for PMOs:

> *You know, what I love is having people who look after*
> *our business for me and who help me drive our strategies*
> *forward – the PMO does both, which isn't what all*
> *departments do …*

And we have already heard from one vice president in the foreword who is very clear about the value of a PMO (with a good PMO leader):

> *My experience of PMOs has been completely positive helping*
> *unify strategic intentions with operational necessities, but it is*
> *a mission that requires a leadership rather than management*
> *approach. Because you are dealing with people and ideas and*
> *future states it does not become real until someone says it is*
> *real and that person might just need to be you.*

4　PM Solutions Research. (2010) 'The State of the PMO 2010'. Research report. Glen Mills, PA: PM Solutions, p. 1. www.pmsolutions.com.

The PMO Acid Test

Do people ask why they should use the PMO and do they know what your PMO does?

You should have marketed the value of your PMO throughout the organization and people should easily access a 'service menu' or what the PMO can do to help them.

3 Being a Successful PMO Leader

In this chapter we take all of the knowledge gained from the stakeholder feedback and assimilate it into a Competency Framework against which PMO leaders can assess themselves.

ONE VISION?

Do we now have a clear view of what a good (and therefore potentially successful) PMO leader is?

Well yes, I think that we do.

Having listened to those voices from four directions: the PMO leaders, the project managers, the employers and the 'C'-level executives, you should, I hope, have a good feel for what it is that you should aspire to and what skills you should either already possess or those you need to work hard to improve.

We heard many good points of feedback such as:

For the PMO leaders from the PMO leaders:

1. One size of PMOs doesn't fit every situation. Rather, flexibility is key to success since PMOs should be closely linked to the business and this demands an evolving approach that moves with the business demands.

2. Balance well between people and process since the PMO

is primarily a people business unit, but one that needs method and process to aid its work.

3. Never be afraid to promote your PMO and your projects since no one else will to begin with. Hopefully, others will soon speak the praises of the PMO but, just in case, talk often and talk loudly and with pride.

4. Act like a business leader, because that is what you are, but don't forget your roots and the roots of the PMO – do have a continued passion for projects.

5. Track the benefits of what you are doing as, not only can you not manage what you don't measure, you also can't direct when you don't know where you are.

6. Be a strong leader, champion your PMOs work, represent your project managers and be honest in the business demands.

For the PMO leaders from the project managers:

1. A PMO is mostly a good thing as it helps bring order to their projects and their lives but more is needed to engage them in their careers and in their skill development, so place some effort in this area to ensure that the project managers continue in their support and belief in the PMO.

2. Don't swamp the project managers with process and method unnecessarily but aim to get the right blended approach. Continually assess if this is the case and adjust accordingly. Process has a habit of accumulating layers over time.

3. Be supportive about projects and project management, back to the 'not forgetting your roots'.

4. Be decisive – it is said that making any decisions is better than making no decision at all.

5. Communicate well to the many, many stakeholders that a PMO has and make sure that any such communication plan is 'alive', that is, that it evolves and changes as the communications needs change and the stakeholder relationship progresses.

6. Use all of those people skills that you should have – projects and process have their place but it is primarily a people thing. Perhaps the 'P' in 'PMO' should stand for 'people'?

For PMO leaders from the managers of PMO leaders:

1. Communicate well, as we have discussed above – do good communication and keep it relevant.

2. Negotiate fairly and strongly, as part of the business it is all about a fair balance.

3. Be an agent of change since this is what projects are all about, delivering change to an organization, and the PMO is the management body for the projects.

4. Demonstrate your self-managing capability by just that, being considerate of the surrounding business elements and making the PMO part of that whilst not being a burden on the business.

5. Believe in the business and the projects. Without this you, the PMO, the projects and the people are worthless.

6. Know the project world by keeping yourself up to date with what is happening, what the challenges are – sharing the pain and the celebrations.

If I overlay the four 'voices', let's see if is the messages have anything in common.

To start with, remember we are trying to identify what it is to be a 'leader' of a 'successful' PMO.

Loud and clear from the combined feedback comes the need for any PMO head to be knowledgeable about projects and project management and have a passion for this type of work.

Be passionate about projects and project management

Being able to communicate well is also critical (as project managers we all know the importance of this skill) and for a PMO leader this means being able to communicate in all directions within and outside an organization, and at all levels – from the 'C'-level senior manager through to the project managers, operational managers, customers, team members and other partners.

Be strong in your communication

Communication is key, as are the two skills of negotiation and of facilitating change.

Negotiate well for your PMO

Creating and leading a PMO is a tricky balancing act with many stakeholders and, consequently, there are many opportunities for resistance, confusion, misunderstanding or bewilderment. Add to this the fact that the PMO is a body of change, overseeing the mechanisms of change (that is, projects), then a complexity can easily occur.

Be enthusiastic in leading change

All of this demands the best of your negotiations and change management skills.

There you have it, some excellent advice on the right skills to be a good leader of a PMO.

And as for the 'successful' part?

Well, just as important as that passion for projects we discussed is the plea to make your PMO exactly that, your PMO – one size does not fit.

109

Don't be afraid to be unique: anything else is probably wrong for you and your business

To be successful, look at what there is out there and then create something that is unique to your businesses needs.

Do that and you will be both successful and a leader.

TAKE ME TO YOUR LEADER

Managers are people who do things right. Leaders are people who do the right thing.

Warren Bennis and Burt Nanus[1]

---

1   Warren Bennis is Professor and Founding Chairman of the Leadership Institute at the University of Southern California, and the author of over 30 books on leadership, including *On Becoming a Leader* and, most recently, *Geeks and Geezers*. Bert Nanus is a renowned expert on leadership and the author

There is, of course, yet another added dimension: that of 'doing all of this with the right people'.

We have heard through our 360-degree feedback what skills are foremost in leading a PMO – and we know that our PMO leadership must include doing the rights things in the right way in the right order and with the right people – but there must be something more?

We have explored that a PMO is not a static thing and must be flexible in its formation and behaviour, must be an agency of change and must align to the strategic business needs.

We discovered how a PMO leader needs to engage and motivate many stakeholders from all levels of an organization.

We have investigated the models and types of PMOs and what aspirations a PMO should have to attain enterprise level and to secure sponsorship directly at the executive level.

of many books on the subject, including *Visionary Leadership*. Now Professor Emeritus of Management at the University of Southern California, he was also Research Director of the Leadership Institute.

All of these features suggest that a PMO will not benefit from being led by a manager but cries out for a leader; someone who has a vision for the project-based organization and the project managers within it.

> *Shallow people believe in luck ... the strong believe in cause and effect.*
>
> Ralph Waldo Emerson

THE PMO LEADER COMPETENCY FRAMEWORK

A typical role-based Competency Framework will have elements covering:

- business;

- personal;

- leadership;

- technology; and

- the core skills of the specific role.

So, as a pertinent example, a Project Management Competency Framework might well look something like this:

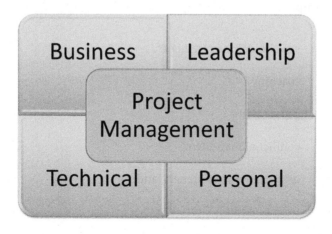

It's useful to break down these competencies further:

Business competencies:

- knowledge of the organization;

- core business application systems and process;

- legal aspects;

- compliance standards;

- human resources aspects; and

- business skills or acumen.

Personal:

- networking and influencing;

- communication – oral and written;

- decision making;

- problem solving; and

- facilitation.

Leadership:

- stakeholder management;

- coaching;

- people skills;

- conflict management;

- organizational awareness; and

- team building.

Technology:

- application environment;

- standards and policies and procedures; and

- personal responsibilities.

Our research on PMO leadership has highlighted the importance of particular interpersonal skills – namely, communication and negotiation. We have also seen that the successful leader needs to have a passion about project management. And finally, to complete the cornerstones of PMO leadership success, an individual should not fear being one of a kind, leading a unique business unit, nor should they be timid about leading change within their organizations.

113

Let's assume that you are a good project manager with a good track record in project delivery and with a solid amount of practical experience behind you – the good and the bad, since a lot of project lessons learned come from the bad.

Let's also assume that you understand your business and its processes and governance; and that you have all of the technical knowledge that you need to do the job.

Finally, let's assume that you are a well-rounded individual with a broad range of personal skills that make you pleasant to work with and productive in what you do.

Let's now focus on those special attributes within the Competency Framework that seem to be so important, over and above the other foundation skills. The ones that all parties to the 360-degree review agreed on.

BEING PASSIONATE ABOUT PROJECTS (AND PROJECT MANAGEMENT)

Projects, and therefore their management, are fast becoming the preferred way for companies to get things done. In a global economy, project-based working will make a company more competitive than the traditional methods of managing work, and the PMO is a key component of this approach.

If you accept this logic, then it follows that all managers need to understand the dynamics of projects, together with the skill and process of project management, in order to make the most out their organization's investments; this is doubly true for PMO leaders.

The good PMO leader must champion project management and project managers across their organization. Their message? That PMOs are:

- good for the business;

- do not threaten the 'business as usual';

- and that change and commercial consistency can exist in harmony.

There's more: the executive needs to be educated in the ways of 'projects', how best to evaluate and initiate, prioritize and resource projects, and how to use the PMO in supporting their strategies for the business.

You need to showcase what the PMO does through newsletters, case studies, lunchtime presentations – whatever works in your business. Co-present with operational business managers to demonstrate what can be achieved by working together. Share information at Board meetings and steering meetings to explain what the PMO is overseeing and delivering. Speak at customer-facing events about the benefits of PMO-based projects.

I don't believe the role of the PMO leader is just a job – it is a mission and a mission that requires passion.

> *One person with passion is better than forty people merely interested.*
>
> E. M. Forster

COMMUNICATE WITH CONVICTION

Demonstrating conviction and self-belief does not mean riding roughshod over anyone else's views and forcing your opinion at every opportunity. It means that when you speak of the PMO and its projects and project managers to all of your stakeholders you should represent what you are trying to achieve for the business in a fair and transparent way.

Effective communication means working out exactly what messages you need to deliver, making use of the most effective communication method for the person (or people) with whom you need to communicate, and delivering your message at the appropriate time. Let me add that, to ensure that you get the right feedback, you need to educate people as to what information you need; how you would like to receive that information and when. Regular project status reports are a great example of this. Just demanding information from your project team and then never explaining what you do with that information (or worse, not actually doing anything with the information that they have worked to deliver to you) will lead to low-quality data that can impact your project. Explaining clearly how data is to be used and what actions and decisions are taken based on that data is far more likely to result in people working harder to supply good information to you.

Communication is a two way process after all.

In brief:

- consider what needs communicating and to who;

- plan the means of communication;

- check that the communication is working well; and

- maintain effective communication channels.

As a PMO leader don't forget the greatest of all skills – listening. Remember the old adage, 'We have two ears but only one mouth.' It will serve you well.

Listen to what people are saying about the PMO and the projects and the project managers. Make the most of positive feedback and make sure you actively investigate when you hear of bad communication, or problems that have occurred through poor communication.

Finally, you need to learn how to communicate (up and down) at all levels within the organization. The PMO must be connected to the business, and that means the commercial business strategy, as well as ensuring value to the business units. You need to be as comfortable in the boardroom as on the factory floor, across all regions that you represent and with all cultures that you encompass.

> *The single biggest problem in communication is the illusion that it has taken place.*
>
> George Bernard Shaw

117

NEGOTIATION[2] FOR THE BUSINESS AND THE PMO

A PMO is still a new concept to most businesses. And most people, as we all know, worry about new things.

The result is that PMO leaders will often face the challenge of dealing with resistance to change. A new PMO needs to find its rightful place within a business and, in doing so, will face challenges:

- it is unlikely to be a business unit that is immediately accepted and understood;

- few people have any history of working with PMOs;

---

2   There may be confusion between the 'advocacy' role and the skill of 'negotiation' when the term 'negotiation' has been used. Negotiation is a dialogue intended to resolve disputes, to produce an agreement upon courses of action, to bargain for individual or collective advantage, or to craft outcomes to satisfy various interests. Advocacy is the active support of an idea or cause and so on – especially the act of pleading or arguing for something. It can be safely assumed that both are required by PMO leaders.

- there are still plenty of people who don't understand the project world;

- it isn't a statutory compliance unit that has to be respected and followed; and

- it may well simply be seen as novel business experiment and, as such, it could be treated as a transitory irritation to business as usual.

So there are plenty of challenges to make life interesting for a PMO leader.

Amidst all of this, you, the PMO leader, will need to work hard to make sure that the PMO is:

- well resourced;

- understood;

- well respected;

- appreciated;

- and most of all – used.

All of this will require skilful advocacy to ensure that the PMO
(a) gets everything that it needs to stand a chance of success; and
(b) is smoothly incorporated into the business of which it is now a key part.

> *In business, you don't get what you deserve, you get what you negotiate.*
>
> Chester L. Karrass

BEING ENTHUSIASTIC ABOUT LEADING CHANGE

Change is tricky and it is tough to get right. Everyone feel uncomfortable when the status quo is threatened and frightened people often react with hostility towards those they regard as responsible for the threat.

As leader of a PMO you represent change in many forms:

- You lead projects. Projects, in themselves, represent change – considerable change – inside and outside the business.

- You are the head of a new business unit that has the authority to reach across boundaries in the business-as-usual set up.

- You may well incorporate the management team's desire for change which is expressed through the delivery of their strategy initiatives.

In other words, change is pretty much what you do and you'll need to be enthusiastic about it. Not least because enthusiasm is infectious, which is something that you can exploit in your mission to make your PMO the best it can be for you and your business. It is said that we are the average of the five people we most closely associate with.[3] So if you are one of those five people closest to others then you have a great opportunity to promote yourself, your work and the PMO. If you present enthusiasm at all (reasonable) times then you really can influence others around you. It is also said that enthusiasm is contagious (but so is the lack of it) so be careful and be positive. At all times, even the difficult times, present what you are trying to achieve in a way that is:

- Positive – as we have seen your enthusiasm can be infectious and engaging with people over the positive aspects of the PMO can only be a good thing.

- Good for everyone involved – listen to people's views and try and identify challenges they face that the PMO may be able to help with.

---

3   'You are the average of the five people you spend the most time with.' – Jim Rohn, motivational speaker and self-help guru.

- The right thing to do – talk about the 'greater good' for the organization and the mid- to long-term benefits of improved project success and strategy alignment.

- Something that everyone should buy into – you need to 'sell' the idea that the future is the PMO and get people on board with the plans that you, and the management, have for the PMO.

Of course you need to keep an open mind and be seen as someone who does consider others' views.

Once change is under way, albeit only stuttering forward, then make that change 'stick'. Kotter[4] suggests this as the last in his eight steps to leading change; ensuring that what has been achieved is anchored in the corporate culture.

After all, making change happen is hard enough but watching what you have achieved disappear just as fast (or probably faster) would not be good.

> *We know that leadership is very much related to change. As the pace of change accelerates, there is naturally a greater need for effective leadership.*
>
> John Kotter

BELIEVING IN UNIQUENESS

Finally we come to the conclusion that your PMO will almost certainly be different to every other PMO in some way, great or small.

---

4   John Paul Kotter (born 1947) is a Professor at the Harvard Business School, and an author who is regarded as an authority on leadership and change. In particular, he discusses how the best organizations actually 'do' change (Kotter and Cohen, 2002). Kotter is the author of 15 books, and his international bestseller, *Leading Change*, outlined an actionable, eight-step process for implementing successful transformations. In October 2001, *Business Week* magazine rated Kotter the number one 'leadership guru' in America based on a survey they conducted of 504 enterprises. In 1996, it was named the number one management book of the year by *Management General*.

If you have led a PMO before then take this as a key learning point:

- The next PMO that you will lead will be different. The people will be different, the projects will be different, and the business will be different; the result of which is that the PMO will be different.

As such you need to proceed in a way that acknowledges that there is no simple, single, out-of-the-box approach to developing a PMO. Yes there are tools you can use and there are applications that you can use but the shape and strategy of the PMO will be unique to the actual situation that you are in.

Remember:

- do things for the right reason;

- consider but don't be influenced by others' emotions;

- know your own opinions, informed by others but formulated by you; and

- be flexible in how you think and in what you do.

Unlike pretty much every other business unit, the PMO will be special in what it aims to deliver to the business and how it goes about delivering it.

As we have already considered:

- Be passionate about what you do, communicate what you do, negotiate acceptance of what you do, and be enthusiastic about what you are leading.

    Don't let anyone tell you that you have to be a certain way.
    Be unique. Be what you feel.
    Melissa Etheridge

The PMO Acid Test

Do people ask many times over where they should go for project information or project help?

The PMO should be the automatic first call for anything project related when project managers or others need some guidance. Make sure yours is easy to access and quick to respond.

4 Starting a PMO

In this chapter we consider how to initiate a PMO in the first place, make sure that it is the best PMO possible, plan for its evolution over time and make sure it doesn't end up of the scrapheap of failed business initiatives.

We also come to terms with the fact that there is no single or simple answer.

I WANT ONE OF THOSE

Building the case for a PMO

Any business case should focus on and define the key problems that the solution should address. In this case it is the investment in a PMO. For any change to take place and be supported there has to be either a 'pain' that needs resolving or a benefit that wants to be achieved – or perhaps a combination of both. For the PMO the 'pain' will be a list of project issues, low quality of deliverables, late delivery, budget overruns and so on. The benefit might include avoiding lost opportunities or accelerating strategic deployment.

You get the picture I'm sure.

Indeed there may be no need for such an argument at all if the business itself understands the value of a PMO and opts to invest in one to support project activity.

It sounds simple, and it can be, but organizations vary in their approach to such matters and you will know your own organization the best. What is essential is that you have the sponsorship at executive level in order that this business case is well received.

Therefore you might consider developing your PMO business case in the following way:

Assessment: During this assessment stage, record all the problems that the organization is experiencing. Make sure that you reach out to all the stakeholders – executive, project owners, sponsors, project managers, partners, customers and business unit leaders. You can do this through interviews and surveys – anyway that you feel is appropriate and generates the information you need from the people that matter. A useful tip is to use quotes from those that you have interviewed, this brings a touch of reality to the business case and added buy-in from those who spoke out.

Also try and quantify the impact of the issues that you are reporting. It helps gain support when people are presented with simple to understand 'consequences' (whether in monetary terms or other) for the issues that you uncover in the assessment.

Don't be unjustifiably negative here – if something is already working well then say so – it is quite possible that an initiative for, say, project management training that is already underway, to be taken under the wing of a new PMO and developed to become more effective.

Benefits: Using the assessment list, develop a benefits statement which will define the value that you believe will be delivered to your organization by the successful implementation of the PMO that you are proposing. (Tip: Make sure that you include some sort of growth plan as a PMO cannot be expected to address all of the problems and provide all the solutions from day one. Start with the most significant needs first and then identify where the PMO's attention will move to in phase two and three and so on. Double check these with the key stakeholders to validate your priorities.)

Consider structuring your benefits under three of the 5 'P's headings:

1. P = People

2. P = Process

3. P = Promotion

4. P = Performance

5. P = Project Management Information System

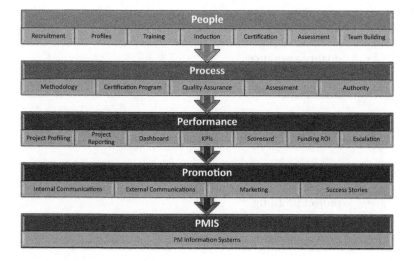

Focus on the 'people', the 'process' and the 'performance' aspects for now.

Think about what benefits your proposed PMO will generate for the following:

The 'People':

- recruitment

- profiles

- training

- induction

- certification

- assessment

- team building

The 'Process':

- methodology

- certification programme

- quality assurance

- assessment

- authority

The 'Performance':

- project profiling

- project reporting

- dashboard

- KPIs

- scorecard

- funding ROI

- escalation

You may prefer to structure in this way:

Project aspect:

- better project performance – delivering on time;

- better project performance – delivering within budget;

- better project performance – delivering to scope; and

- improved customer satisfaction – project output meets agreed customer expectations.

Business aspect:

- improved efficiency – through standardization of operations and methods;

- higher utilization – through better resource allocation and capacity planning;

- accurate time to ROI – through faster and better quality project status reporting (progress, risks, issues, changes and so on);

- improved project initiation – through a more realistic prioritization of project work;

- better decision making – through the combining of business 'silos' into one business representation; and

- raised professionalism – through the development of a project management community.

You should also consider the type and model of PMO that you are proposing to lead and articulate the options that are possible and preferable. Stakeholders should understand the opportunities that a PMO can offer as well as the various means of a PMO working within and for a business.

Take a moment at this point to consider the likely evolution plan for the PMO – perhaps you intend to start at departmental level and scale up for the enterprise in the future, once the PMO has gained experience and a track record of success (and the business is ready to invest at that level).

Remember you need to win over hearts and minds through your business case and you need to build the 'need' to a level that is critical. One way to achieve this is to:

- link the business case to the 'problems' that the PMO can address;

- add in the 'benefits' of investing in the PMO;

- and don't forget to remind the audience of the 'implications' of not moving ahead with a PMO.

All of this must, in the minds of the decision makers, be greater than the combined 'cost' and 'risk' of accepting this change proposition together with the perceived 'pain' of such change being carried out plus any 'hidden' concerns that your stakeholders may have.

Build that case and you have good chance of winning your argument – you will be given the green light for your PMO.

Getting started

There are two scenarios that new PMO leaders will face when they first pitch for a PMO.

You may be starting from nothing at all; there is nothing in place within the organization, no project managers, no reporting structure, nothing. This is the least likely scenario given that most companies who invest in a PMO will already have some project-based activity in place. Of course, a 'green field' investment for a PMO is possible in a new start-up.

The second, and more likely scenario, is that the PMO creation is an evolution of the existing project-based activity and, as such, you will inherit whatever project infrastructure and people are already in place.

My PMO survey reported that the large majority, 78 per cent, of project managers who expressed a view had experienced the development of a PMO in companies that already had a project management team. In other words, the PMO leader would have needed to take what was in place and craft a PMO from the raw materials.

Was the PMO created before or after your organization had a project management team?

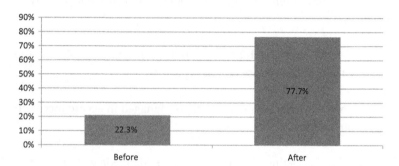

Let's spend some time considering the steps a new PMO leader might take when setting up a PMO in an established project environment. It is critical to begin by utilizing what already exists but to also understand what it is that exists (good and bad). What is the reality of the foundation that you are trying to build the PMO on?

If you don't already have a detailed business case your first step should be to develop a robust one.

Baselining for success

It is said that you can't manage what you don't measure and this is absolutely true of projects. So it is important to start with some basic benchmarking activities.

Consider the following three elements:

1. assessment of project management maturity;

2. input from the project managers; and

3. the importance of honesty.

How mature is your organization's project management?

You may consider gaining some objective and external guidance in running an assessment of project maturity. There are a number out there and they all tend to align to a generic maturity model on five levels.

> Level 1: Initial (chaotic, ad hoc, individual heroics) – the starting point for use of a new process.

> Level 2: Managed – the process is managed in accordance with agreed metrics.

> Level 3: Defined – the process is defined/confirmed as a standard business process, and decomposed to levels 0, 1 and 2 (the latter being Work Instructions).

> Level 4: Quantitatively managed.

> Level 5: Optimizing – process management includes deliberate process optimization/improvement.

Each of these maturity levels includes a number of Key Process Areas which characterize the level:

*   goals

*   commitment

*   ability

*   measurement

*   verification

Whatever approach to such a maturity assessment you take: (a) there will be benefit from understanding in more detail (beyond your business case, unless such a maturity assessment was part of that case development) what the PMO has in the form of experience and skills and project discipline and, well, maturity; and (b) you will have something that will be accepted as an objective and informed baseline that you can measure progress against in the coming months and years.

Listen to your project managers' concerns.

Reach out to your project managers and ask them for their thoughts and feedback.

Keep it simple, you are only looking to find out their mood and the major issues that they consistently face. You might ask, for example, for the three things that cause them the most difficulty in their daily jobs.

From this information you can summarize and report the most common themes, the big issues if you like, and you can then consider some specific remedial plans against each of these issues.

There are two critical points here: (a) make sure that you feedback the findings and any plans of action to the project managers; and (b) run the survey every year; project managers will always find at least three things to report back on but hopefully you will see the top three themes changing as maturity progresses and your actions plans come to fruition as the PMO evolves.

Bring out your dead

Finally, and depending upon your internal project reporting systems, you may want to consider some sort of process to get to the truth about all of the projects that you, as the PMO, now own.

Consider some sort of amnesty for a defined period during which project managers (and others) can open up and state the reality rather than the 'modified for the executive' version of the health of their projects, without fear of blame.

Don't be afraid of the truth, understanding precisely how ill (or well) the patient is makes for a better cure and a more effective recovery plan.

Don't consider a red traffic light as a disaster. Red is the colour of opportunity.

Sure, for a PMO leader, glancing across their project and portfolio dashboard red usually means ... well it usually means trouble of some sort and trouble means that there will be work to do. So red is unlikely to be welcome.

On the other hand, the one thing that you need from the PMO members, the project managers, is honesty. If they can honestly share the state of play in their projects with you then you can establish yourself as being on their side. And, just as importantly, if you know the true state of things then it also means that the PMO can offer the right level of help; conversely, if you don't know the truth, then you're in no position to provide help before matters get too critical.

Beyond the baseline

Once you have all the necessary baselining information to hand you can start the process of PMO development.

Have a look at the following areas:

The 'People':

- recruitment

- profiles

- training

- induction

- certification

- assessment

- team building

The 'Process':

- methodology

- certification programme

- quality assurance

- assessment

- authority

The 'Performance':

- project profiling

- project reporting

- dashboard

- KPIs

- scorecard

- funding ROI

- escalation

There are technical applications that the PMO can use, such as a project management information system or a professional services automation tool, project dashboard and so on but my advice is, don't rush in too early. There are many, very useful tools out there but you should work first with what you have and then, once you have the insight and understanding of what the projects, the PMO and the business actually need, you can make a better and more informed selection of which tools to use.

And please don't forget to market the PMO!

Market, market, market!

Remember, an approved business case is no guarantee at all that all of the business managers believe the PMO is a great idea. You may know it is but you now have to win others over to your way of thinking.

Take every opportunity that you can to market, promote and sell the value of the PMO. In time you may choose to develop a PMO services menu (what the PMO does and how to request such a service) but in the early days offer your help wherever there is an opportunity. A proactive approach helps open doors to the PMO and it will start people talking in a positive way about the PMO work ethic and capability. This can be done through any way you think is appropriate.

- newsletters (project management community ones and company ones);

- showcases (presentations, lunch time sessions, case studies and so on);

- Intranet presence;

- post-project reviews (PMO attendance and write-ups);

- project manager of the year awards;

- project of the year awards;

- marketing 'goodies' with the PMO 'brand';

- project manager peer recommendations (about the PMO value);

- executive declarations;

- offering 'project management for non-project managers' training outside the PMO/project community;

- blogs; and

- podcasts.

And much more.

A little marketing and self promotion goes a long, long way.

Don't be shy. You believe in your PMO so help others to see its value as well.

AND I WANT A BETTER ONE

So here you are, leading a successful PMO and all is well with the world.

Did you plan a phase two? Was there a next step that the business expected? Is there a next step that the business is now requesting?

If the answer to any of these is 'yes' then now is the time to move onwards and upwards (according to your plans); perhaps extending to an enterprise-level PMO or including the company with an outreach PMO, for example.

If not then now might be the time to consider such an expansion (and by expansion I don't mean 'empire building').

As a starting point, why not just revalidate the current support for the PMO and also revalidate the business need. You can do this by reviewing the history of the PMO activity and considering successes and improvements. As ever, the better the foundation you have for building the PMO, the better.

Taking the PMO pulse

Perhaps it is not so much a matter of moving to phase two but more of wanting to improve what you already have in place; modest improvements can be just as valid as major new developments.

On the other hand, maybe things aren't going quite as well as you had hoped?

Typically you will need to return to the business case. Here are some questions that you might ask of yourself and of the PMO:

- Has anything significantly changed in the business that requires an adjustment by the PMO?

- What is the view, within the business, of the value of the PMO?

- Are there any key opponents to the PMO operation?

- Are the methods you have established well adopted and adhered to, and have recommended improvements been acted upon?

- Has the level of project maturity risen?

- Are project managers reporting the same issues as before?

- Has there been a change in the PMO sponsorship role(s), personnel or approach?

- Has project 'health' improved or stagnated?

- Is the PMO approach the right one?

- Is the PMO model the right one?

You may need to survey the PMO stakeholders to understand in more detail what it is that needs extra effort and focus. Alternatively, it may be that you just need to get together with your PMO team and revisit the PMO purpose. Don't forget to check out the PMO Leaders' Checklist in the appendices as well.

MOVING UP THE FOOD CHAIN

Let's return to that satisfying point in time where you are leading a successful PMO and all is well with the world. This may be because you are proving to be a great leader of a great team or it may be as a result of an improvement programme).

Either way you are there, ready for the next step. So what is the next step?

Well you may have, as we have already suggested, planned for that in the original business case. In this case you will need to:

- reconfirm that the business is still committed to this and the time (and budget no doubt) is available; and

- enact the PMO 'next step'.

If you have not planned such a second phase in the PMO then you will need to go back to the business case process and seek approval for what you wish to do next.

So you now need to:

- consider your options (go back to the type and approach options for any PMO);

- assess the cost and the benefits for the option or options you elect to present to the business;

- build a detailed justification for this option(s);

- construct a plan of action;

- present to the key stakeholders; and

- evolve ...

The Outreaching (Supplier) PMO can offer the Customer PMO
guidance in PMO set up and PMO Governance as well as resources
from the (Supplier) PM Community

The most likely evolution of the PMO will be to move from a departmental level to an enterprise level of operation, if it is indeed an internal PMO that we are talking about. This allows the PMO to position itself at a strategic position within the organization and to operate in a way that ensures that projects are sanctioned based on their strategic business alignment rather than any other measure. Executive support for an enterprise PMO is an enormous benefit in progressing in all areas of responsibility (back to the 5 'P's).
In some organizations the enterprise PMO will have local or departmentally-based PMOs reporting in to it and will manage the projects accordingly.

There will, of course, be a significant expectation that an enterprise PMO will positively impact the organization as a whole.

The same is true of an external enterprise PMO but the strategy will be that the external customers are treated in a consistent, standard and professional manner globally, regardless of their contact points throughout the supplier organization.

AVOIDING THE DODO EFFECT

Walters' definition of project Dodo: 'A project that will only fly for a very short distance at a time and only upon application of a speeding massive boot to the arse. We all know it will become extinct very soon.'

You may think of your PMO as a project but you surely don't want it to be a project of the Dodo variety?

Apart from the special-purpose PMO there is not a specific expectation that any other form of PMO is a temporary business unit. That said, there is absolutely no expectation that the PMO is a permanent business support unit either.

What is true is that the time of the PMO is now and that there is an accepted need for PMOs to aid and drive the increasing project-based business that organizations are experiencing (more than experiencing really, often they are encouraging such project activities) and in many cases to aid the realization of strategic business objectives.

However, it is important for any good leader to regularly validate that what they are leading and what they are doing is still relevant.

We all speak of going the way of the Dodo and, as such, we, as PMO believers and champions, do not want our PMOs to become obsolete (at least not until their time has passed). So:

- keep vigilant;

- Constantly validate the business view of the PMO;

- market and promote the PMO value;

- challenge project activity outside of the PMO's remit;

- get as close to the business strategy as is appropriate for your PMO; and

- demonstrate constant project-based improvements (people, process, customer satisfaction and so on).

So what happens if the PMO 'goes the way of the Dodo'?

Well, in many ways there will be a reversal of the creational process of the PMO, but perhaps with less control.

Projects and project managers

Project managers will be out of a practice and will be, most likely, moved back in to departments and smaller business units. This could result in an in-balance of resources in these business units. There may also be less stringency applied to methods and process and quality. Objectivity will be reduced as will escalation levels and recovery resource capability.

The induction process for new project managers may be lost as could any support or mentoring capability which could lead to less-prepared project managers engaging with key projects. Linked to this will be a fragmentation of the 'knowledge repository' of a larger project community as well as less focus and effort on maintaining methodology.

Business and customers

Certainly project management will become far less aligned with any strategic business priorities. There will been an almost complete disconnect between sanctioned projects and such strategy as departments will pit themselves against departments not for the greater good but for the local success and reward.

The engagement model with external customers will be weakened as the standard 'language' of communication and behaviour will no longer be common in its approach.

Visibility of project activity will be harder to track and even harder to substantiate.

It seems very clear that if you believe in PMOs (and believe in your own business) that you would not want any of this to happen. So keep it relevant. Always.

The leadership interview – the death of a PMO

Derek is, or was, the leader of an experimental PMO within a mid-sized electronics organization in the Asian market.

His background was 12 years of project management linked with business development activities with key customers.

Interview

Peter: Derek, perhaps you can start with explaining how and why the PMO came about and how you ended up as the PMO leader?

Derek: Sure, as part of the project management team in our company it was felt by many of the project managers that there were just better ways of doing all of the stuff that we did, day to day. Generally it was a pretty pressured working environment with high customer demands – demands fed more often than not by our sales team. Our projects were directly linked to new product lines that customers committed to.

Peter: So whose suggestion was the PMO?

Derek: I guess that came primarily from the project managers, well at least some of us, just wanting to make some progressive change to make the projects run that much smoother.

Peter: And you got elected as the leader?

Derek: Yes, eventually. We had to do the big sell to the business that a PMO was a good thing and find a sponsor to help make it happen. It wasn't as if this was a major cost investment, more of a shift in focus of activity to ensure better results later on.

Peter: And you found a sponsor?

Derek: Yes we did, one of the executives picked up on the buzz about PMOs and came on board pretty fast.

We planned out methodology development and training, put together a simpler project dashboard, set up a helpline for all of the project managers to use and intended to move our people along some certification path eventually.

Peter: That sounds pretty good so what happened? How long did the PMO last?

Derek: It lasted less than 18 months in total, about three months to plan and then running for 12 months before a fragmented collapse I guess. The first problem was the sponsor left very early on in the process; he was pretty career minded and moved on to a better role, bigger company. So that was a blow but we were up and running by then and thought it would be OK.

Peter: And it wasn't?

Derek: No, we surveyed our project managers and they were pretty happy with what was going on, they generally felt that at the very least they had a community to belong to, that they were not alone any more, and that someone cared.

Peter: They had a voice?

Derek: Yes. But the executive team didn't see the value add for this effort, and by effort we were only talking of a reasonable percentage of time that all the project managers contributed. Plus a small cost for additional training. Our belief was that this cost would be recovered many times over in future project success.

Peter: But you weren't given the time to demonstrate this?

Derek: No. The hard times hit, as they hit everyone, and all departments costs were closely scrutinized and guess what? The PMO was seen as an overhead that the company could survive without.

Peter: What happened?

Derek: An announcement went out that the PMO was to be ended and we lost a handful of project managers (along with others in the business of course). I believe that not only did the executive not appreciate what we could deliver but that other departments, also under threat of resource cuts, directed managements thoughts in the direction of the PMO as some form of self-defence.

Peter: So other business units were not sold on the PMO value story either?

Derek: I guess not.

Peter: What happened to you then?

Derek: I was lucky as with my experience I was moved back to being a project manager.

Peter: And the PMO was a failed experiment in the minds of the executive team?

Derek: Sadly yes.

Peter: So what do you feel you might have done differently to perhaps given the PMO a better chance in those very difficult circumstances?

Derek: I think the key was that the PMO came from the project community and was not seen as a business strategy initiative. Given time I am sure that this would have been the case with the PMO successes linking to the business strategy and that would have been a really good thing. As it was, the PMO was just seen as a stand-alone overhead and just something that the project managers wanted and benefitted from.

Peter: So you still believe in PMOs?

Derek: Yes I do but I would definitely approach my next one in a different way. Start with the business and link to the projects.

> ## Make sure the business owns the PMO and believes in the PMO initiative

Peter: Thanks Derek, great insight and I hope your next PMO experience is a much better one.

THERE IS NO HOLY GRAIL

It is apparent that there is no specific 'holy grail'[1] for a successful PMO; there is no single solution that I can lay down for you to follow.

Just looking back at all that we have explored as far as PMOs are concerned shows us the complexity of structure and operation.

Remember the five 'types' of PMO?

1. a departmental PMO

2. a special-purpose PMO

3. an outreaching (supplier) PMO

4. an external (customer) PMO

And the models of an enterprise PMO (internal and external).

Remember the four 'modes' of PMO?

---

1   The Holy Grail is a sacred object figuring in literature and certain Christian traditions, most often identified with the dish, plate or cup used by Jesus at the Last Supper and said to possess miraculous powers. The connection of Joseph of Arimathea with the Grail legend dates from Robert de Boron's Joseph d'Arimathie (late twelfth century) in which Joseph receives the Grail from an apparition of Jesus and sends it with his followers to Great Britain; building upon this theme, later writers recounted how Joseph used the Grail to catch Christ's blood while interring him and that in Britain he founded a line of guardians to keep it safe. The quest for the Holy Grail makes up an important segment of the Arthurian cycle, appearing first in works by Chrétien de Troyes. The legend may combine Christian lore with a Celtic myth of a cauldron endowed with special powers.

1. supportive;

2. controlling;

3. directive;

4. and a blended version.

Remember the 'virtual' and the 'physical' PMO options?

And the 'maturity' aspects?

There is so much flexibility and therefore complexity in the operation and structure of any PMO that almost all things are possible.

145

We said way back at the beginning of the book that your PMO will be special to you and your business and that is so true.

So I am sorry if you were looking for the single 'answer' that just isn't possible to provide. Instead all I can offer is a vision of what your PMO might look like and consideration of how you might go about creating your PMO, and how you should think about leading your PMO in a successful way that makes it the best PMO for your business and absolutely relevant to your business.

The PMO Acid Test

How can you improve the PMO's work and profile, its performance, its acceptance and its role in your company?

How can you do this? You need to think and plan and act; like a leader.

A GOOD PMO IS NOT MEASURED BY THE PMO LEADER

No, it can only be measured by the project managers that they lead. A good PMO leader will take the massed skills and knowledge of such project managers and take them in the right direction for the business and for the projects.

Just think of the project managers you have in your PMO, add up the number of years that they have had all together in project management. Chances are that you won't personally have anywhere near that level of experience, so use what you all can share and lead them to success.

Two quotes from Ray Kroc[2] are apt here:

> *You're only as good as the people you hire' – or in the case of the PMO, the PMO leader is only as good as the project managers that they inherit, recruit, develop, mentor, encourage and lead.*

And

---

2   Raymond Albert 'Ray' Kroc (1902–1984) was an American businessman who took over the small-scale McDonald's Corporation franchise in 1954 and built it into the most successful fast food operation in the world. Kroc was included in Time 100: The Most Important People of the Century and amassed a US$500 million fortune during his lifetime. He was also the owner of the San Diego Padres baseball team starting in 1974.

> *'The quality of a leader is reflected in the standards they set*
> *for themselves' – so as a PMO leader set the standards for*
> *yourself that you expect others to follow, lead by example.*

And never forget the project managers.

One great way that you can do this is to join in the celebration
of International Project Management Day (see Appendix 4) – a
perfect vehicle to shout out loud what the PMO and the project
managers have achieved and a great way to thank everyone for their
contribution.

THE ACID TEST

Are you being successful in promoting and leading your PMO?

Did you take the five question 'acid' tests and how did you score?

Who

> *Call up your CEO and then count the number of seconds*
> *before he recognizes your name ...*

If you are really connected to the business, at the right level and
with the right profile, then your CEO will know you and your PMOs
work.

You don't have to start with the CEO, you can try this out moving
up the organization level by level – who at two levels above you
knows you and the work that the PMO performs? For those that do
say 'thanks' and for those that don't; well tell them about it.

What

> *What happens when you call up a project manager? Do you*
> *get straight through or do they adopt an avoidance strategy?*

A call from any member of the PMO should be a welcome event and
not something to hide from or fear.

Consider if there are certain individuals or teams or departments that are resistant to what the PMO is trying to achieve. Ask yourself why this is and plan a charm offensive to demonstrate that the PMO is their friend.

When

> *When was the last time that a project manager contacted your PMO asking for some form of help?*

If this has not happened in some time then perhaps your PMO is not as accessible and open as you may wish it to be?

Run a survey or open session to gain some insight into the reasons for non-contact with the PMO. It may link to the 'what' question above, that is, fear of the PMO, or it may be just a lack of awareness. Go out of your way to help key people, regardless of if it isn't really in your PMO remit – by winning influential supporters the word will spread about the PMO being a 'go to' group.

Where

> *Do people ask many times over where they should go for project information or project help?*

The PMO should be the automatic first call for anything project related when project managers or others need some guidance – make sure yours is easy to access and quick to respond.

Market what the PMO does, create a menu of service items that the PMO can deliver 'off-the-shelf' and advertise this tirelessly.

Why

> *Do people ask why they should use the PMO and do they know what your PMO does?*

You should have marketed the value of your PMO throughout the organization and people should easily access a 'service menu' or what the PMO can do to help them.

Success stories really help here with proven benefits of PMO involvement – invest your time in developing some and get people outside the PMO to write them or at least validate them.

How

And finally question number six – the 'how':

> *How can you improve the PMO's work and profile, its performance, its acceptance and its role in your company?*

How can you do this?

You need to think and plan and act.

You need to lead.

Good luck, I hope this book has been of some help.

5 The Final Frontier

Now for some final thoughts on the future of the PMOs that we are all leading (I do hope successfully or at least now on a clear path to success).

The PMO was born out of a need to improve project success and link the project activity to the business needs. However, since they were created from change, should they not also anticipate changes in the future? We must not be complacent even in our period of success and acceptance.

Versions of the first three of the following articles were first published by PMI®[1] under their 'Voices on Project Management' blog.[2]

A PMO IS NOT FOR LIFE

Just as a project is not for life, 'A project is a temporary endeavour undertaken to create a unique product, service or result' (we all know the PMBOK[3] definition I am sure), and a programme is

---

1 The Project Management Institute (PMI) is a non-profit professional organization for the project management profession with the purpose of advancing project management.
2 'Voices on Project Management' (PMI) offers insights, tips, advice and personal stories from project managers in different regions and industries.
3 *A Guide to the Project Management Body of Knowledge* (PMBOK Guide) is a book which presents a set of standard terminology and guidelines for project management. The Fourth Edition (2008) was recognized by the American National Standards Institute (ANSI) as an American National Standard (ANSI/ PMI 99-001-2008). The PMBOK is developed by the Project Management

not for life either, 'A programme is a group of related projects managed in a coordinated way ...' (again drawing from the PMBOK definition), then, as the home for project managers and projects and programmes, should we not consider the evolution of the PMO in the same light?

The PMO has become the place to be for many project managers and is perceived, mostly correctly, by the businesses that they support, to be of significant value in driving the quality of the projects they oversee in an increasingly project-based world. It is also a pretty good career move for many experienced project managers wanting to progress up the ranks.

However, there is a danger. If the PMO is seen as a body or unit that has no end goal then it will become purely a home for operational activity. If it is seen as only the home of process (methodology) and the body of control (policing) then it will become as exciting as working in ... well I had better not pick on an actual back office function but I am sure you understand what I getting at.

Back with the PMBOK, it contrasts projects with such operational work by stating that 'operations are ongoing and repetitive'. I am not saying PMOs will only be around for a very short time, I'm not, I am merely suggesting that, out of all of the business units and because of the nature of what they contain, they must continue to evolve and ensure that they are really creating value.

Project management is an exciting job as well as a challenging one. As project managers we all need help, and a good PMO focusing on the people, the process, the performance of the projects and the promotion of project successes is increasingly critical. The PMO has emerged as a way that executives can feel more at ease with the project activities within and without their companies.

Leading a PMO is an equally exciting job but anyone working in such a role has a responsibility to consider the end game. We typically know what it is that we are trying to improve, resolve,

---

Institute (PMI) which is the world's leading not-for-profit membership association for the project management profession, with more than half a million members and credential holders in more than 185 countries.

correct and direct, but I don't believe that this should be done in a way that creates a permanent need over the heads of project managers. They are smart people who just need some help along the way and, in time, with guidance and support from their PMO, they should become self-sufficient and a community that can aid future generations of project managers. What we really must avoid is the deliberate removal of a subset of project management skills and the replacement of these skills within a permanent overhead community – a PMO.

It is said that operations end when they stop delivering value, and projects end when they do deliver value. The PMO should aim to end when there is no longer a need for it to exist because it has delivered the value and that lack of need should be engineered in to its strategy.

153

A PMO IS NOT THE ONLY ANSWER

The PMO is one of the fastest-growing concepts in project management today, but it's not the only answer.

The PMO was born to aid the project manager. Surely then, the PMO (and, as a direct result, you) would benefit if there were a parallel organization for the technical managers, consultants, architects, design specialists, gurus of the world of application configuration and so on.

The PMO is not and should not be an isolated body talking only to the project managers. It should be one of many business units leading the delivery of company strategy.

Align the PMO to a single technical body, no matter what it is, and then align the two through a common process or methodology.

Think about your own in-house project methodology for a moment. Is it just for project managers or does it extend to integrate the technical tasks? Does it recognize the non-project management roles and responsibilities? Does it involve the technical deliveries and control mechanisms? It should.

If you have a common method, have you trained each team in a way that they both respect and understand each other's skills and duties? Have you done so in a way that ensures the highest level of communication? You should.

When your business assesses the value, benefit and simply whether a new project should go ahead at all, it won't just be the project manager's view that gets the budget approved, will it? So align the technical gurus and the project gurus as one to ensure that the lowest risk and highest ROI projects are commissioned.

Perhaps the future is the perfect pairing of a PMO with a TMO – a technical management office. It may be that the TMO is formed as a separate entity but closely works alongside the existing PMO? Or even that the PMO embraces and includes the TMO function?

The specifics of how a PMO/TMO relationship would take shape are up to what's best for your own organization but perhaps it is the future. What do you think?

A PMO IS NOT THE MOTHER OF ALL PROJECT MANAGERS

Just to remind ourselves, there are typically three styles of PMO – directive, supportive and controlling.

The directive PMO actually manages the projects by using the project management team that is part of the PMO. The supportive PMO generally provides help in the form of on-demand expertise, templates, best practices, expertise and so on. The controlling PMO offers guidance and discipline with a desire to improve by standardizing on the process and the method.

The reality is that very few PMOs are just any one of these types but rather they are a blended mix of two or three of the PMO types. In a recent survey I undertook the results from 590 PMOs across the world showed that 80 per cent were not directive PMOs but a mixture of supportive, controlling and with 33 per cent blended, that is a mix of activities depending upon individual project need.

So the majority of PMOs seem to avoid the direct self-managing of projects.

In my own PMO we aim to avoid direct ownership of projects except in a few specific cases such as if the project is in a location where there is low local project capability or the project has gone badly wrong (and in this latter case we aim to 'own' the project for as short a time as possible, always developing a transition plan back to the original project manager if at all possible). We are a blended PMO with a strong focus on support and with an offering of controlling to those project managers that need our help.

So the PMO should not generally be considered the 'mother of all project managers' but rather the body that helps develop the best project managers out there facing the in-house stakeholders or the external customers on a day-to-day basis. The ones on the coal face, the ones that are experiencing the meeting of theory and practice.

- A PMO can replace a deficient project management process with a standard and best practice.

- A PMO can, most likely, save considerable costs against project management overheads, such as training, certification and so on.

- A PMO can create a community of project managers and bring teams and processes together to maximize the shared knowledge and engender a spirit of cooperative working.

- A PMO can market its overall successes and spread the word about what a great job its project managers are doing.

- A PMO can work closely with a business to align projects with strategy.

- A PMO can be a fantastic source of knowledge and a great safety net.

- A PMO can do many, many things.

- And a PMO is a really good idea.

But, at the end of the day, the project responsibility and ownership still lies with the person best equipped to do the job: the project manager.

Let's not forget the project manager.

GIVE ME A 'C'

I have seen in the companies that I have worked for, and I am sure that you have all seen it as well, the special ones amongst us that are on a fast track up through the organization destined for the hallowed ground of 'C'-level appointment.

There is nothing wrong with that at all. They experience the company as broadly as possible with time spent in finance, sales and marketing and even sometimes in services perhaps. They get first-hand experience of the components of the businesses that they will one day lead and this is a really valuable preparation. These are the ones identified as having future leadership potential and any company will invest in such people for their joint futures.

Sadly I have yet to see a future 'C' work their way through the project arena, the PMO, the project management practise. It seems as if, when it comes down to it, that the project side of the business (as opposed to the operational side of the business) is maybe a little less important, a little less attractive?

There is a danger of course in putting a non-project person in charge of projects.

A comment from my recent PMO survey summed it up with: 'The management in charge of the PMO are highly experienced operational managers, each with a significant and solid track record. Unfortunately that expertise does not translate into projects where the deadlines, delivery management and interaction between different role-players are significantly more acute than in operational management.'

So perhaps the 'C' is not immediately destined for the PMO leadership role but surely there is a critical need for such future leaders to understand the nature of their ever increasingly project-based activities.

Take action all of you PMO leaders – talk to the 'powers that be' and to the fast-track talent development agencies in your companies and open up your PMO with an invitation to 'come on in and enjoy the experience'. In the long run it will only benefit the PMO (and the organization).

> *Actions, not words, are the ultimate results of leadership.*
> Bill Owens

Appendix 1
PMO Leaders' Checklist

Status	PMO Leaders said:
	One size doesn't fit all, flexibility is key
	Balance well between people and process
	Never be afraid to promote your PMO and your projects
	Act like a business leader but have a continued passion for projects
	Track the benefits of what you are doing
	Be a strong leader

Status	Project Managers said:
	PMO is mostly a good thing as it helps bring order to their projects and their lives but more is needed to engage them in their careers and in their skill development
	Don't swamp with process and method unnecessarily, get the right blended approach
	Be supportive about projects and project management
	Be decisive
	Communicate well
	Use those people skills

Status	Managers of PMO Leaders said:
	Communicate well
	Negotiate fairly and strongly
	Be an agent of change
	Demonstrate self-managing capability
	Believe in the business and the projects
	Know the project world

Appendix 2
An Insight into the
Minds of Your
Project Managers

Through the survey, and beyond the obvious which we have already explored, there are definitely other lessons that I have learned and ones that I am happy to share with you regarding working with project managers.

As mentioned, the survey attracted 823 respondents – people willing to spend a short period of time sharing their experience with me for the sake of this book and PMOs in general. There was a bribe (incentive) in that people who completed the survey could register for a free copy of my eBook *The Lazy Project Manager*. So the scene was set and it was all 'carrot' and no 'stick'.

As you can see from the chart on the next page, as we move through the questions from one to eight there was a significant drop off in submissions.

Question 1 was the 'How long have you been in a PMO?' one and instantly it proved all too much for one person who bailed out from the survey.

Question 2 was the 'What is your role in the PMO?' and the number held steady for this along with Question 3, 'What is the focus of your PMO? Internal/external projects and so on?' So far so good.

Then at Question 4, 'Was the PMO created before or after your organization had a project management team?' something interesting happened. I lost 16 per cent of the audience. Now bearing in mind we were still on simple 'radar button'-style click questions,

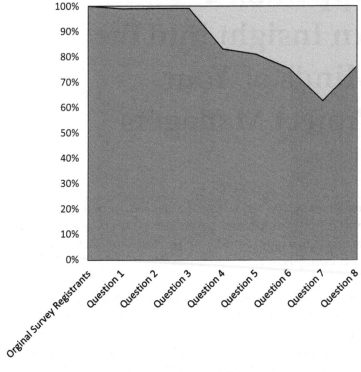

Attention span of a project manager

perhaps the answer as to why so many left me, 140 in total, was more to do with the fact that the survey moved to a second screen here.

I had pre-warned people that there were only eight questions and the first three were hardly challenging but nevertheless I lost a significant number of people here, which was a real shame.

Never mind – onwards we go.

Question 5 was the harder one, 'How do you feel as a project manager working under a PMO – looking at the following aspects rate your current experience against the time when there was no PMO?' with seven sub-questions: support, training, success, quality, career, process and personal experience. Plus each sub-question had a choice range of six possible answers: much improved, better, no change, worse and much worse plus the 'I have always worked in the PMO' one. So a decision matrix with many, many possible combinations.

However, the survey takers stayed with me here, perhaps because they felt that this was the important question? Anyway, only 17 more had had enough by now and quit the survey.

However, then came Question 6 all about 'What type of PMO did you work in?' Another new survey page managed to lose me 25 per cent of respondents from the start of the survey and 7 per cent from the previous question. Again a simple 'radar button' click me to vote question but not enticing enough a question to keep all the people happy and interested.

Which brings us to the last two questions, both of which were 'type in your thought' questions. No radar buttons now but free format text fields. Challenging.

Question 7, 'Since your organization has had a PMO in place what is the general view of the success of the PMO?' resulted in a further 17 per cent drop off but this did recover to a degree with the final question. Question 8 was, 'What do you feel are the most important aspects of being a successful leader of a PMO?' and the numbers increased here with a 22 per cent rise in responses.

This was possibly due to two reasons. One was that Question 8 was a mandated/please answer one whereas Question 7 was not and secondly perhaps people had more of an opinion about the last question?

There were of course a number of people who played the game by just entering random text or numbers or just the 'no comment' option but these were very few.

So thank you once again to all who answered even just the one question, the input has been invaluable for this book.

And lessons learned?

Well there are two I think.

First:

A free something, in this case a copy of *The Lazy Project Manager* ebook, works wonders at getting people interested so always make what you are doing attractive in some way. 550 people downloaded the eBook in the end.

And second:

The attention span of Project Managers is limited. Just making them turn to a new screen or page makes them drift away in numbers and find another 'pretty' to focus their attention on. As with all communication, make it as simple as you can without losing the message and as focused as you can to the individual that you want to receive the message. For a project manager it is best to keep it to one page maybe?

Appendix 3
PMOSIG

The survey that formed the basis of the results featured on pages 70 to 83 was undertaken in July to October 2010 using the web-based Survey Monkey tool and promoted through Twitter and LinkedIn, as well as The Lazy Project Manager podcasts, blogs and website www.thelazyprojectmanager.com, and through the support of the PPSO SIG[1] (now PMOSIG).

 The PMOSIG is a not-for-profit organization which is owned by its members – it is not aligned with any methodology or industry. Membership is free and open to anyone employed or interested in the management and support of portfolios, programmes and projects in any industry.

Two conferences a year are organised, one in the spring (one day) and the other in the autumn (two days). The content is a mixture of expert speakers, member speakers (who are experts in their own PMOs), structured networking and workshops, creating a varied blend of learning, sharing, fun and problem solving. There are also informal local group meetings held late afternoon and early evening in key locations. Members come away from the conferences better informed and better connected, and with a whole host of

---

1   Born in December 2000, the PMOSIG was originally launched as the PPSO SIG; ten years later they continue to hold conferences and networking events that allow like-minded professionals to get together. The PMOSIG is a not-for-profit organization which is owned by its members – it is not aligned with any methodology or industry. Membership is free and open to anyone employed or interested in programme and project support in any industry. http://www. pmosig.co.uk/

ideas to put in place back at their own PMO. The feedback from
conference delegates is always overwhelmingly positive, which is a
great indicator of the value of the group.

PMOSIG (formerly PPSO SIG) started ten years ago and was
originally created to satisfy the new demand for PMO professionals
to link up, share experiences and move the profession forwards.
More recently, industry recognition has given the group a solid
reputation and a springboard to become more and more involved in
forming how PMO thinking and practice evolves.

There are development plans in place to create a more sustainable
and long-term group that will be seen as a force to be reckoned with
in the world of PMOs – very exciting times are ahead, and all PMO
professionals can be part of the journey.

To join PMOSIG, please visit the website at http://www.pmosig.co.uk/
to sign up; you can also find much PMO-related material and
conference material from the last few years.

Appendix 4
International Project
Management Day

Earlier in the book we discussed the critical point that a great
PMO leader never forgets their project managers. It was suggested
that one great way you can do this is to join in the celebration of
International Project Management Day – a perfect vehicle to shout
out loud what the PMO and the project managers have achieved and
a great way to thank everyone for their contribution.

Well, we can now hear from the founder of International Project
Management Day – Frank Saladis:

INTERNATIONAL PROJECT MANAGEMENT DAY
(ALWAYS THE FIRST THURSDAY IN NOVEMBER)

The building you're in right now as well as the one you slept in last
night and every movie you've ever watched. The medical breakthroughs
that are saving thousands of lives every week and every product ever
invented and every business and organization that ever formed.

The roads we travel on, the public utilities that support our cities,
the emergency plans that go into action during crisis.

The Internet and all of the IT applications that advance our world,
our education and our global connectivity are all tangible projects
and proof of the power of project management.

You, as project managers and programme managers, should take
great pride in the work you do. You may not do it alone, but project

managers are, without question, the world's change makers – even more so humanities change makers.

International Project Management Day is a day to celebrate and appreciate the power of the profession, and to individually say thank you to project managers everywhere.

Hi, I'm Frank Saladis, and in 2003 I started thinking about the need to have a day specifically designated for project managers. An International Project Management Day to promote appreciation for project managers, their teams and their achievements; and to promote the value of project management as a method for achieving success in any industry.

On each International Project Management Day educational events and gatherings happen around the globe in recognition of the value of project management. More specifically it is a day to say 'thank you' to the millions of project manager who dedicate themselves to achieving project and organizational success.

Some groups hold appreciation events, others attend presentations about project successes and others attend receptions honouring project teams. Others simply take a few moments to say 'thanks' with a smile, a card and a handshake.

One important part of International Project Management Day is to connect with other project managers like yourself around the world. So we say 'welcome'. You may say 'Bienvenida', 'Willkommen', and 'Bienvenue' as we reach out to project managers around the globe.

Through your participation, you're helping realize a vision for International Project Management Day in which all businesses, all managers, clients, your own PMO and even your family will see and appreciate what you do.

This celebration is meant to give you a sense of pride, and to motivate you and others to make positive advancements in project management methods, techniques and practices. I would like to directly challenge each of you to do five things in support of International Project Management Day.

These five things are:

1. Do something positive for yourself to increase your sense of personal power and self-worth.

2. Take the time to say thanks to your project managers and team members. Do something organizationally to recognize and appreciate those working on projects with you.

3. Participate locally in project management events.

4. Create or join a regional mission to enhance the public relations of the industry.

5. Finally, identify actions you can take to build your international network and become an international ambassador of project management.

DO SOMETHING POSITIVE FOR YOURSELF

Here are some ideas about what you can do personally. Think of the projects you have been assigned to in the past year. What challenges did you overcome? What successes were achieved?

*   Make an appointment with an executive or senior manager and discuss the strategic value of project management.

*   Encourage a colleague to consider a career in project management.

*   Help an aspiring project manager by offering advice and encouragement.

*   Invent new best practices in project management.

*   Be proud of your work.

*   For the experienced project manager, consider becoming a mentor to a new or aspiring project manager. Mentoring

enhances our feelings of self-worth and helps others achieve their dreams and your mentorship will ensure continued growth of the profession.

- Plan for your personal professional development.

- Read project management books (such as this one on *Leading Successful PMOs*), attend classes and commit to achieving a project management credential.

Project management exists in a fast-changing environment and you need a plan to stay ahead by expanding your personal skill set.

I encourage you to create a personal plan that emphasizes core values, project management competencies and development of your leadership abilities. You will always be ready for what is just beyond the horizon. Believe in yourself. You're the first and most important part in the five-part challenge.

170

TAKE THE TIME TO SAY THANKS TO YOUR PROJECT MANAGERS

- The next challenge is to do something within your organization.

- Schedule a recognition event and showcase successful projects.

- Highlight the contributions of your PMO.

- Create a sense of pride in project management in your organization.

- Take the time to communicate and celebrate your team's successes.

- Acknowledge other project managers and team members working for, with and around you. Ideally we should do this every day, but for International Project Management Day be extra generous with your acknowledgement.

We all need to develop organizational cultures where projects consistently come in on time, within budget and according to specification. We strive to build cultures where conflict is solved through facilitation, effective listening, idea generation and respect for each person's point of view.

We work towards an organizational culture where leadership is clearly demonstrated at every level and the focus is on effective performance, employee well-being and where the customer is considered a top priority.

Gandhi said, 'Be the change you want to see in the world' – become a change agent, or an advocate for change, through the application of project management. Project managers are the drivers of change.

PARTICIPATE LOCALLY IN PROJECT MANAGEMENT EVENTS

If you look around your community you will see numerous projects near completion so take a moment to appreciate the work involved.

- Locally, attend a professional association meeting such as a Project Management Institute (PMI) chapter meeting. PMI has chapters around the world. You could also meet with other professional groups such as the International Project Management Association (IPMA).

- Schedule a recognition event for project managers in your community. Everyone can appreciate the new building projects, road projects, events and business start-ups in your area.

- Publish an article in a local newspaper or create a newsletter. Perhaps form a team, or join a team to participate in a community improvement project.

JOIN A REGIONAL MISSION

Think of yourself as an ambassador for project management and help promote your industry's public relations. Work with your state, province or territory governing body and encourage them to recognize and proclaim the first Thursday in November as International Project Management Day. In the past, several cities and states have issued proclamations, including the Mayor of New York City, who annually declares the International Project Management Day as a formal day of recognition.

- Connect with project management colleagues outside of your community and help create an international bond with project managers in other countries.

- Observe and learn about projects that have contributed to history or are changing the world. The genesis for change is awareness.

Change – it's what project management is all about. Building your awareness of projects around the world will help you imagine greater possibilities and inspire new ideas. I encourage you to learn about other cultures and seek opportunities that provide you with exposure to internationally diverse teams.

Whenever possible travel. Mark Twain said, 'Travel is fatal to prejudice, bigotry and narrow-mindedness.' So travel – reach out, connect and always learn.

Look back in history at the significant projects that the world admires and appreciates. The effort to reach out internationally will help all of us better understand and appreciate the values of different cultures. There are many projects around the world that are inspiring and testimonials to the power of project management. The Louvre in Paris for example, the pyramids of Giza, the Taj Mahal in India, the Piazza del Duomo of Milan, the Great Wall of China, the Opera House in Sydney, Australia and many, many more.

BUILD YOUR INTERNATIONAL NETWORK

Project management can be described as one part imagination, one part inspiration, one part motivation and one part determination. In other words, all of the qualities of a strong leader.

The Internet is our connection to the world. Reach out to project managers in other countries – especially those that work in the same industry that you do. Use social networking to connect with project managers in other industries – for example, there are many LinkedIn groups covering PMOs and project management, programme management, agile methods and so on .There is both PMI and APM and on Twitter there is the community #pmot (project managers on Twitter); Facebook connects many project managers as well. You will notice that we all share similar skills so do not be afraid to share your ideas, contribute to their information needs and learn from them.

Together we can create an international network of project management knowledge champions.

CALL TO ACTION

I've challenged you to take actions on a personal, organizational, regional and international level today.

To continue on this mission your leadership is required. You, the project manager, have a place among the world's leaders. Leadership and change are bonded together. Change is what we accomplish through leadership.

John Maxwell said, 'A great leader's courage comes from passion, not position.'

This is the right time to renew your passion for project management, or should I say project leadership. It is your courage and willingness to accept challenge that demonstrates the power of the profession.

I hope this call to action will help you realize your efforts will live into the future and you are connected, needed and appreciated. You, the project manager, are truly indispensible to your organization's success.

I therefore encourage you to celebrate International Project Management Day with your partners in project management around the world. I hope you'll plan to do this on an annual basis.

But remember:

- projects are in progress every day of every year;

- take the time to acknowledge your project teams;

- remain conscious of your leadership position;

- and always seek new ways to add to the value of project management.

It's up to you. Project managers see their teams as astronomers see the skies; filled with stars.

Thank you – Frank Saladis.

FOR MORE INFORMATION

The International Project Management Day is intended to encourage worldwide project-based organizations or organizations who utilize project management methodologies to schedule some type of recognition event within their organizations or coordinate locally with others to truly demonstrate appreciation for the achievements of project managers and their teams.

International Project Management Day is always the first Thursday in November.

The website www.internationalpmday.org provides you with the contacts, information and resources to help you plan your organization's International Project Management Day. It has resources that can help you get your area's International Project Management Day proclamation completed or to help project managers in your area or PMO receive acknowledgement and appreciation for their work.

Appendix 5
PRINCE2

WHAT IS PRINCE2?

PRINCE2 (PRojects IN Controlled Environments) is a process-based method for effective project management.

PRINCE2 is a de facto standard used extensively by the UK Government and is widely recognized and used in the private sector, both in the UK and internationally.

The method PRINCE2 is in the public domain, offering non-proprietorial best practice guidance on project management. PRINCE2 is a registered trademark of OGC.

The key features of PRINCE2 are:

- Its focus on business justification.

- A defined organization structure for the project management team.

- Its product-based planning approach.

- Its emphasis on dividing the project into manageable and controllable stages.

- Its flexibility to be applied at a level appropriate to the project.

PRINCE2 HISTORY

PRINCE was established in 1989 by CCTA (the Central Computer and Telecommunications Agency), since renamed the OGC (the Office of Government Commerce).

PRINCE was originally based on PROMPT, a project management method created by Simpact Systems Ltd in 1975. PROMPT was adopted by CCTA in 1979 as the standard to be used for all Government information system projects.

When PRINCE was launched in 1989, it effectively superseded PROMPT within Government projects. PRINCE remains in the public domain and copyright is retained by the Crown. PRINCE is a registered trademark of OGC.

PRINCE2 was published in 1996, having been contributed to by a consortium of some 150 European organizations.

Appendix 6
Manager or Leader?

Leadership can be defined as 'organizing a group of people to achieve a common goal'. The leader may or may not have any formal authority to do this.

Leadership can also be defined as the 'process of social influence in which one person can enlist the aid and support of others in the accomplishment of a common task'.

Kurt Lewin[1] and colleagues identified different styles of leadership:

1. autocratic

2. participative

3. laissez faire

AUTOCRATIC OR AUTHORITARIAN STYLE

Under the autocratic leadership style, all decision-making powers are centralized in the leader, as with dictator leaders.

They do not entertain any suggestions or initiatives from subordinates. The autocratic management has been successful as it

---

1   Kurt Zadek Lewin (1890–1947) was a German–American psychologist, known as one of the modern pioneers of social, organizational and applied psychology. Lewin is often recognized as the 'founder of social psychology' and was one of the first to study group dynamics and organizational development.

provides strong motivation to the manager. It permits quick decision making, as only one person decides for the whole group and keeps each decision to himself until he feels it is needed to be shared with the rest of the group.

PARTICIPATIVE OR DEMOCRATIC STYLE

The democratic leadership style favours decision making by the group, for example, leader gives instruction after consulting the group.

The democratic leader can win the cooperation of their group and can motivate them effectively and positively. The decisions of the democratic leader are not unilateral as with the autocrat because they arise from consultation with the group members and participation by them.

LAISSEZ FAIRE OR FREE REIGN STYLE

A free reign leader does not lead, but leaves the group entirely to itself, for example, a leader allows maximum freedom to subordinates, that is, they are given a free hand in deciding their own policies and methods.

Different situations call for different leadership styles. In an emergency when there is little time to converge on an agreement and where a designated authority has significantly more experience or expertise than the rest of the team, an autocratic leadership style may be most effective; however, in a highly motivated and aligned team with a homogeneous level of expertise, a more democratic or laissez faire style may be more effective. The style adopted should be the one that most effectively achieves the objectives of the group while balancing the interests of its individual members.

EXERCISE

Here is an exercise that you might wish to run with your PMO team.

Many people confuse or merge the different attributes of management and leadership. This exercise enables people to understand the differences. Anyone can lead, inspire and motivate others. Leadership is not the exclusive responsibility of the CEO, directors and senior managers. Encourage staff at all levels to aspire to and apply the principles of good leadership, and the whole organization will benefit. Everyone, in their own way, can be a leader. In fact organizations which have poor leadership at the top actually provide a great opportunity for ordinary staff and junior managers to take responsibility for leading, inspiring and helping to develop others. Don't wait to be led – be a leader yourself!

Here is a list of many things that managers and leaders do. Either issue the list or, preferably, make (or ask the team to make) separate cards or post-it notes for each word/phrase which can be given to a group or team. Then ask the participants to identify the items that are associated with managing and those that are associated with leading. Groups of over five people can be split into teams of three, to enable fuller participation and a variety of answers for review and discussion. Each team must have their own space to organize their answers. Different teams can be given different items to work with or a whole set for each team. Manage the quantities and scale according to the situation and time. Note: To shorten and simplify the exercise remove items for which similar terms exist, and combine other similar items, for example reporting and monitoring. If shortening the list ensure you keep a balance between management and leadership items.

Reporting	Decision making	Implementing tactics
Monitoring	Mentoring	Resolving conflict
Budgeting	Negotiating	Giving constructive feedback
Measuring	Keeping promises	Accepting criticism and suggestions
Applying rules and policies	Working alongside team members	Allowing the team to make mistakes
Disciplining people	Sharing a vision with team members	Taking responsibility for others' mistakes
Being honest with people	Motivating others	Formal team briefing
Developing strategy	Giving praise	Responding to emails
Consulting with team	Thanking people	Planning schedules
Giving responsibility to others	Being determined	Delegating
Determining direction	Communicating Instructions	Reacting to requests
Explaining decisions	Making painful decisions	Reviewing performance
Assessing performance	Appraising people	Time management
Defining aims and objectives	Recruiting	Nurturing and growing people
Doing the right thing	Counselling	Team building
Taking people with you	Coaching	Taking responsibility
Developing successors	Problem solving	Identifying the need for action
Inspiring others	Selling and persuading	Having courage
Running meetings	Doing things right	Acting with integrity
Interviewing	Using systems	Listening
Organizing resources	Getting people to do things	

If using post-it notes or another method enabling items to be stuck to a wall you can suggest that items be placed on either side of a vertical line or string or different flipcharts (attach headings 'leadership' or 'management' to each side), in which case the strength of association that each item has with either heading can be indicated by how close each item is positioned in relation to the dividing line (items that are felt to be both managing and leading can be stuck on the dividing line or third flipchart).

The significance and importance of each item can be indicated by how high up the wall it is positioned. This creates a highly visual 'map' of management and leadership competencies. The review discussion should investigate reasons and examples for why items are positioned, which can entail items being moved around to each team's or whole group's satisfaction and agreement.

Here's the list sorted into suggested categories for the facilitator to use when reviewing the activity.

The answers are not absolute as context and style can affect category. There is certainly a justification for some of the 'managing' activities to appear in the 'leading' category if the style of performing them is explained as such, for instance 'reporting the performance of the team in a way that attributes praise and credit to the team' would be an activity associated with leadership, whereas 'reporting' is a basic management duty. You can add tasks, duties, responsibilities and behaviours to the list, and/or invite team members to add to the list with ideas or specific examples, before the exercise. To shorten and simplify the exercise remove items for which similar terms exist, and combine other similar items, for example reporting and monitoring.

Managing	Leading
Reporting	Team building
Monitoring	Taking responsibility
Budgeting	Identifying the need for action
Measuring	Having courage
Applying rules and policies	Consulting with team
Discipline	Giving responsibility to others
Running meetings	Determining direction
Interviewing	Explaining decisions
Recruiting	Making painful decisions
Counselling	Defining aims and objectives
Coaching	Being honest with people
Problem solving	Developing strategy
Decision making	Keeping promises
Mentoring	Working alongside team members
Negotiating	Sharing a vision with team members
Selling and persuading	Motivating others
Doing things right	Doing the right thing
Using systems	Taking people with you
Communicating instructions	Developing successors
Assessing performance	Inspiring others
Appraising people	Resolving conflict
Getting people to do things	Allowing the team to make mistakes
Formal team briefing	Taking responsibility for mistakes
Responding to emails	Nurturing and growing people
Planning schedules	Giving praise
Delegating	Thanking people
Reacting to requests	Giving constructive feedback
Reviewing performance	Accepting criticism and suggestions
Time management	Being determined
Organizing resources	Acting with integrity
Implementing tactics	Listening

Appendix 7
Some Further PMO Reading

Business Driven PMO Setup: Practical Insights, Techniques and Case Examples for Ensuring Success
Author: Mark Price Perry
Hardcover: 528 pages
Publisher: Roundhouse Publishing Group (7 Jun 2009)
Language: English
ISBN-10: 1604270136

The Program Management Office Advantage: A Powerful and Centralized Way for Organizations to Manage Projects
Authors: Lia Tjahjana, Paul Dwyer and Mohsin Habib
Hardcover: 272 pages
Publisher: Amacom (1 Nov 2009)
Language: English
ISBN-10: 0814414265

The Complete Project Management Office Handbook
Author: Gerard M. Hill
Hardcover: 752 pages
Publisher: Auerbach Publications; 2nd edition (6 Sep 2007)
Language: English
ISBN-10: 1420046802

The Program Management Office: Establishing, Managing and Growing the Value of a PMO
Author: Craig J. Letavec
Hardcover: 388 pages
Publisher: J Ross Publishing (1 April 2007)

Language: English
ISBN-10: 1932159592

Emotional Intelligence: 10th Anniversary Edition; Why It Can Matter More Than IQ

Author: Daniel Goleman
Hardcover: 384 pages
Publisher: Bantam; 10 Anv. edition (26 Sep 2006)
Language: English
ISBN-10: 055380491X

Gower Handbook of Project Management: Fourth Edition

Editor: Rodney Turner
Hardcover: 912 pages
Publisher: Gower Publishing (24 Jan 2008)
Language: English
ISBN-10: 0566088061

Gower Handbook of Programme Management

Author: Geoff Reiss, Malcolm Anthony, John Chapman, Geof Leigh, Adrian Pyne and Paul Rayner
Hardcover: 738 pages
Publisher: Gower Publishing (24 Oct 2006)
Language: English
ISBN-10: 0566086034

Appendix 8
Some Useful PMO Blogs and Podcasts

Here are some useful links that will lead you to more information about successful PMOs and offer some great insight into what the world is thinking about PMOs right now.

ESI: http://www.esi-intl.co.uk/blogs/pmoperspectives/

BOT International: http://www.botinternational.com/thepmopodcast.htm

Mel Bost: http://melbostpmoexpert.com/

PM Solutions: www.pmsolutions.com (The State of the PMO)

IIL: www.iil.com

Planview: http://www.planview.com/docs/Planview-2008-PMO-2.0-Survey-Report.pdf (The PMO Survey)